OF A

WOMAN

Marriage, Motherhood, Ministry, and Money

SHERABIM J. CURVIN

After The Storm Publishing
GO THROUGH TO GET THROUGH...THE STORM

ISBN-13: 978-0692770269
ISBN-10: 0692770267

AFTER THE STORM PUBLISHING, LLC
A Division of Peace in the Storm Publishing, LLC
39 Myrtle Avenue #2
North Plainfield, NJ 07060

Visit our Website at
www.afterthestormpublishing.com

Table of Contents

DEDICATION

I dedicate this book to my mommy. Now that I am a wife and a mother over the age of 40, I truly understand the many sacrifices that you made for my siblings and me over the years. You did a lot for us, often putting your own desires on hold. I appreciate you now more than ever and I am grateful for your unwavering love and support. You will always be my "Nettie."
Love,

Sheri

ACKNOWLEDGMENTS

To my Lord and Savior Jesus Christ, for entrusting me with your words and wisdom to write this book. Thank you for choosing me to be one of the voices that you would use to provide encouragement, inspiration, motivation, instruction, and deliverance into the lives of my sisters in Christ.

To my loving husband, Ewan Curvin. Thank you for your unwavering support. You always encourage me to pursue my dreams and the visions that God has placed in my heart. I appreciate your patience and your commitment to our family. Thank you for putting up with me. I know that I am not the easiest "nut to crack."

To my son, Emmanuel Curvin. You have added unspeakable and unimaginable joy and gladness to my life. You are my inspiration. I thank God daily for choosing me to be your mother. You are a breathtaking gift, and I will treasure you always.

To my pastor, Bishop Anthony Gilyard, thank you for your counsel and your listening ear. Our last talk is what birthed the courage in me to pursue publishing this book. I love and respect you to the highest.

To my parents, I could not ask for a greater mother or father. You have always been there for my family and me. Your support and godly example of marriage and family will rest with me always.

To my biological sisters Joddice Dickerson and Keraya Jefferson, you are more than sisters. You are my friends and I appreciate and love you both. You both have always been great examples of strength and fortitude to me. We are each other's personal comedians.

To my spiritual sisters Darenda Mays, Karleen Hull, Sophia Garcia, and Helen Jackson, thank you for being you and for your continuous push for me to become all that God has ordained for me to become. Thanks for listening. Thanks for talking me "off the edge," when I've threatened to jump. God truly sent you into my life.

To my publisher, Sharel Gordon-Love, thank you for choosing my manuscript to be a part of the After the Storm Publishing family. I appreciate our talks, and your continuous encouragement. You are a great inspiration.

FOREWORD

Oh what a blessed day it was, when our Almighty God Creator of the Universe paid attention to the needs of Adam in the Garden! God knew that every creature on earth had a partner except for Adam, and he would need a woman to assist him and be his companion. Thus Eve was formed by the hands of our powerful God, to bless Adam's life. But we know Eve was deceived by the serpent to do what God told Adam not to do.

In our lives, Rich Queens, we must totally understand how needed and valuable we are, but we must also know the influence we can have, not only on the men in our lives, but the children, too. We are being observed 24 hours a day 7 days a week of our actions and deeds!

So we need to seriously nurture our Vertical Relation-SHIP with the Father and the Holy Ghost on a daily basis through prostrate prayer, time meditating on the Word and operating in the Fruit of the Spirit in all areas of our lives (especially at home), in order to be a Help and not a hindrance to our Families. What an honor, ladies, it is to have been Chosen by God to be the Kingdom Destiny Partner of your Divine current or future Husband from God, and to be the "Kingdom Professor/Developer" or Divine Parent of your Children, to Push them from the invisible to the visible, to Release their GREATNESS to the World for God's Glory... never take this for granted - what an honor it is. Be grateful NO matter what, for many would LOVE to be in your shoes.

I am extremely proud of one of my Spiritual Daughters, Evangelist Sheri Curvin, who has been tremendously used by God to impact many single women living across the United States! From the time I connected with her, she has taught women to live a sanctified life before the Lord, and to give of themselves to Him first before thinking about marriage. She not only taught this, but she has lived it even to this day (now being happily married)!

This powerful book, The Heart of a Woman – Marriage, Motherhood, Ministry and Money, is sure to truly empower many Women for Generations to come. She shares her own journey from being single to now being married and is transparent about the good and bad decisions she made, and the detriment of not forgiving others and yourself from the past. The instructions that she gives to Mothers is priceless and so valuable because just a few days ago, a young lady I know on Facebook shared she was considering suicide (and she is due to deliver twins in a couple months)! Wow, I am so truly proud of Evangelist Sheri for obeying God to RELEASE this Book from God to the nations for many need it NOW. Also, her wisdom shared with Wives about Marriage being a Gift and also how to be a better steward of the Money God and their Husbands have entrusted in their care, is life-changing.

I am looking forward to sharing this book with all of the Spiritual Daughters/Sons my husband, Bishop Willie Bolden, and I have across not only the United States, but the World for the Glory of God and for the enhancement of Kingdom Marriages everywhere!

I want to leave this thought with you, Rich Queens (Rev. 2:9 NLT and Ez. 16:13 NLT). Be sure to make God proud of everything you say and do, especially to the awesome Divine Husband He has blessed you with. If you wouldn't say or do something to God that you are planning to say or do to your Mate, then don't find yourself doing it to each other - for God is watching and you will be dealt with (Matt. 25:40)!

Honor God daily by the way you honor each other and I guarantee you your Marriage, Motherhood, Ministry and Money will soar like never before. God Bless You all!

Pastor Rhonda A. Bolden
The Well of Fort Wayne
RhondaBolden.com

Preface

I wrote this book because, as a Christian wife, mother, professional, and minister, I began to experience the pressure of trying to manage life perfectly. There were times that I found myself feeling guilty simply because I wanted a break from it all. God had blessed me with all of things that my heart desired, so why was I struggling to stay afloat? After conducting some honest soul searching, I found the answer. The answer was quite simple. I had allowed all of things that my heart had desired to become my central focus. Without realizing it, I had ejected God from sitting on the throne of my heart and allowing Him to guide and to direct me as a wife, as a mother, as a professional, and as a minister. I was trying to do it all on my own without His wisdom and strength. I forgot that the Scripture clearly states in **Psalms 127:1 (NLT**)

Allow God to lead you in EVERY aspect of your life!

"Unless the LORD builds a house, the work of the builders is wasted."

The result was a drained woman who began to operate robotically. However, one day the awesome and magnificent God that I serve, reminded me of this book that he had embedded in my heart 15 years ago while I was still single. When He brought it back to my memory, I began to write as He put things into my spirit. As I wrote each sentence, paragraph, and chapter, God began to settle my spirit and to show me where I had gotten off course and the steps that I needed to take in order to regain spiritual, psychological, emotional and social balance. He let me know that He is concerned about everything that concerns me, but I have to ensure that my priorities and motives line up with His Word.

Women, we do not have to allow ourselves to become burned out by the many responsibilities that we have to manage. We can effectively manage all of what is required of us with vigor and vitality if we honor God and allow Him to lead us. God is intimately aware of the concerns that weigh on each of our hearts. He is just waiting for us to trust Him with our heart completely.

Chapter 1

Heart of a Woman

Heart of a Woman
Scripture Foundation:
Proverbs 4:23(NLT)
"Guard your heart above all else, for it determines the course of your life"

Heart Conditions

If you really want to get to know a woman, all you need to do is spend a few moments engaging in open and honest dialogue with her. Within those few moments, I guarantee you that she will reveal the essence of her heart to you. By the end of your conversation, you will be able to discern whether or not she is trustworthy, a liar, sane, or crazy. Jesus said in **Matthew 12:34 that,** *"for out of the abundance of the heart the mouth speaketh."* The United Sates War council advertised it like this during World War II *"Loose lips might sink ships!"*

The condition of a woman's heart defines her. It is in her heart that she houses her thoughts, desires, dreams, aspirations and creativity. Her spiritual, relational, social, emotional, and financial perspectives are embedded in her heart. The health and quality of her heart determines the tone of her life.

When a woman's heart is mishandled, abused, misunderstood, ignored, overlooked and ultimately broken, it can propel her into a cyclonic state of confusion which prevents lucid thinking and the ability to make sound judgment. Her vision becomes

Your thoughts affect the quality of your life!

obscured, causing her to become incapable of maintaining a sustained life of progress and success. Her positive self-esteem becomes jeopardized and she becomes prone to emotional and mental meltdowns, and if not properly treated, can result in breakdowns.

Many of us have personally experienced and/or encountered women who have suffered from a bleeding heart. Oft times, the broken-hearted woman displays characteristics of bitterness, anger, and/or depression. Likewise, she may be prone to relationship instability, job instability, and bad habits such as overeating, shopping, sexual promiscuity, alcoholism, drug usage or a host of other self-destructive behaviors.

In contrast to the broken hearted woman is the woman whose heart has been encouraged, lifted, cherished, nurtured, appreciated, respected, applauded and ultimately strengthened. This healthy hearted woman is a conduit of love and positivity and is capable of empowering the lives of each person that she connects with. She has a clear vision for her life. She fully understands her purpose in the plan of God and diligently walks in her calling without determent. She is the personification of the woman described in Proverbs 31.

The Most IMPORTANT thing you can ever do...is to GUARD YOUR HEART!

Women of God, our heart is the center of our consciousness. Our thoughts, which fuel our behavior and our drive for life, reside here. **Proverbs 4:23 states:** *"Guard your heart above all else, for it determines the course of your life."*

As women, we must become guardians of our own heart. It is our responsibility to ensure that bitterness, resentment, regret, forgiveness, and negativity remain absent from our psyche. We become guardians of our heart by critically examining what and who we choose to invest our treasure in.

Investment Choices

Most of the women that I know personally will give of their time, money, resources, and love unselfishly. They will give until they have nothing else left to offer. Unfortunately, many of these same women have found themselves suffering from broken-heartedness as a result of not

Ask yourself is this person, place or thing worth my investment!

receiving back what they put out. Despite our good intentions, sometimes as women, we invest our hopes and dreams in the wrong people and in the wrong institutions. When our expectations are unmet, the depth of disappointment can overwhelm us to the point that we resign to never give again.

Matthew 6:21 states, *"Wherever your treasure is, there the desires of your heart will also be."* This scripture teaches us that we must carefully choose who and what we invest our heart, hopes, dreams, and our expectations in. If we place our hope, or our treasure, in the wrong thing, then we put our heart in jeopardy. Our whole outlook on life can become marred as result of misguided heart investments.

- ✓ Singles invest their hope in marriage completing them. Should marriage fail to occur, many lose heart in the faith and the fairness of God.

- ✓ Wives invest their whole heart, soul, and mind into their marriages, forgetting that this investment is the greatest commandment and it is exclusive to our Lord, according to **Matthew 22:37.** These same wives experience inconsolable grief when the marriage does not meet this weighty expectation.

- ✓ Mothers struggle with a sense of failure and disappointment should their children stray from the teachings and examples of morality and social responsibility that she invested in them. While other mothers contend with a sense of uselessness after the children grow up and move on with their own lives. As mothers, we tend to forget that we should commit our children into the capable hands of our Lord as Hannah did. **(I Samuel 1:22)**

✓ Women in ministry become burnt-out and contemplate resigning from their posts due to the opposition received from the enemy, as well as from people. Women in ministry tend to forget the caution given to us by the Apostle Paul in **Romans 12:7,** *"Let us wait on ministry."* Sometimes as ministers, we don't wait to hear from God expressly concerning what we should or should not involve ourselves in.

✓ Professional women become consumed with achieving success and financial security and inadvertently mismanage their priorities. This can result in grave disappointments should the efforts go unrealized. We forget the wisdom of our Savior in *St.* ***Matthew 6:33 which He stated,*** "Seek the Kingdom of God above all else, and live righteously, and he will give you everything you need."

The result of all of these misplaced priorities is a community of baffled and directionless women, who begin to question Gods love, concern and fairness. When we invest our heart in the wrong places and receive disappointing results, we tend to question the validity of the Bible, and our ability to hear God speak to us accurately.

Women, I assure you that everything that matters to us matters to God. He is concerned about our desire and need for marriage, motherhood, ministry and money. However He reminds us as He did the children of Israel in **Exodus 20:5**, *"I the Lord thy God am a jealous God."* He will not tolerate occupying second position in our lives. He wants to be the center of our consciousness at all times.

A Christ Centered Heart

When God sits on the throne of our hearts, the unpredictability of life will not shatter our faith in God's sovereignty. Allowing God to take His rightful place as number one in our lives increases our capacity to endure suffering. Maintaining a healthy and accurate perception of God allows us to emerge from all of our trials with flawless integrity and grace.

When God is our source for all things, we will never become confused about who He is and who we are called to be. God wants us to invest our entire heart and soul in the fact that His will is flawless. He wants us to not only pray as Jesus instructed us to in the Lord's

Prayer, "*...thy will be done on earth as it is in heaven,*" but *He also wants us to accept that His will is perfect.* **(Matthew 6:10).**

Accepting the perfection of God's will means that we will not subject ourselves to comparing the quality of our lives with our peers. Instead, we will embrace the Apostle Paul's

Who sits on the throne of your heart?

perspective which is to learn godly contentment in every stage of life **(Philippians 4:11).**

Prior to fully embracing the essence of a woman's heart, we must first understand why God created us. Women, we are a divinely and uniquely created as a gift to mankind. **Genesis 2:18** records God's intention for our existence. We were created as a gifts that are capable of providing companionship as well as the talent, intelligence, intuitiveness, and fortitude necessary to subdue the earth **(Genesis 1:28).**

This chapter's foundational Scripture teaches us that we must protect our heart because it determines the course of our life. How do we keep our heart healthy and Christ centered so that we live the most successful life possible? The most effective way that I have found to accomplish this is to committing to praying for the condition and motives of my heart on a daily basis.

As simple as this sounds, it is not always easy. It is not always easy because when we really submit to God in prayer regarding our heart condition, He will actually show us the condition of our heart. For example, I had developed a very bad habit of judging the goodness of my heart by my outward deeds (i.e.: I was very active in church ministry, etc.). However, I failed to remember that the scripture warns us in **Samuel 16:7 that**, *"Man looketh on the outward appearance, but the Lord looketh on the heart,"* I can reflect on many times, prior to praying this prayer, I thought I was in good shape. However, once God showed me what He actually saw on the inside, I had to do a lot of repenting and changing! God showed me over the years that my motives for doing things in His name were plain wrong! I did them to acquire a sense of validation of my anointing for myself, and not really doing them to bring glory to Him. He has shown me over the years that I was angry, bitter, and resentful regarding my upbringing and that I needed to let those things go so that He could "bring me up" to the status in Him and in life that He desired to. God couldn't release me into greater things until I released some of the pain and negative emotions that I had housed in my heart since my childhood.

On the same token, God has also shown me some good things about my heart. He showed me that I genuinely have a concern for the women in the Kingdom of God and that I have a desire to see them excel in every area of life. He let me know that if I emptied out all of the negativity that I had been holding on to for so many years, He would allow me to effectively minister to the women in His kingdom.

Women of God, as much as we love the Lord, "life happens." Loss, pain, separation, loneliness, betrayal, and abandonment can absolutely happen to us. However, we do not have to allow these experiences to pollute our life perspective. I have learned that by embracing a spirit of forgiveness, it aids in maintain a healthy perspective on life.

When we find ourselves struggling to forgive, then we have to approach God honestly in prayer about the person(s) or things that's troubling us. Sometimes, the person that we struggle to forgive the most is ourselves. Instead of learning from our mistakes and bad decisions, we lament over them to the point that it paralyzes our progress. This has been a major stumbling block for me. I am learning how to accept the fact that "I DID IT!" I accept the fact that I cannot change my past decisions, but I can certainly ensure that I do not repeat the mistake in my future. Ladies, it is time for us to forgive ourselves and let it go! The fact is that God already knew what we were going to do prior to us committing the folly, and He had already decided that He was going to forgive us once we repented. God has forgiven us the moment that we repented, yet we still hold it against ourselves. We do this in ignorance of the scripture in **Romans 8:1** which states: *"So now there is no condemnation for those who belong to Christ Jesus."*

Women, God requires us to forgive everyone who has wronged us, including ourselves, if we expect Him to issue His forgiveness to us **(Matthew 6:15)**. God has the power to administer a healing balm to our hearts that will erase any and all scars that we have acquired in this life.

What is troubling your heart? Is it fear? A lack of confidence? Self-pity, anger, grudges, envy, conceit, jealousy, laziness, disobedience, or hatred? Whatever is causing you to have spiritual congestive heart failure, I encourage you to make it a point of prayer. Let's pause for a moment and pray.

Let Us Selah and Pray

(Personalize the prayer by filling in the blank spaces)

Father God, in the name of Jesus, please look on my heart and show me what you see. Where you see attitudes and motives that displease You, I repent and I ask for Your forgiveness. I pray the same prayer as King David did when his heart became corrupted by the wrong attitude, please "Create in me a clean heart; and renew within me a right spirit." (Psalms 51:10). Please take out my old heart with its old attitudes and motives and create in me a heart that is free from_____ (add your troubled heart condition) anger, unforgiveness, bitterness, and resentfulness. Please fill my heart with the Fruit of the Spirit which is love, joy, peace, longsuffering, gentleness, goodness, faith, meekness, temperance: against such there is no law, as stated in Galatians 5:22. Lord Jesus, please help me to have a heart like you had. The focus of your heart was always to be centered and focused on the things that brought glory to your Father (Luke 2:52).

Lord, I want to live the best life possible. I know that in order to do this, I have to guard and protect my heart with every fiber of my being. I can only do this with your help. When situations arise that would threaten my healthy heart, infuse me with your strength to overcome them as opposed to them overcoming me. I know I can do all things through Christ which strengthens me (Philippians 4:13) and this includes keeping a clean and pure heart before You. Lord, I thank you for hearing my prayer and I am looking forward to seeing these changes manifested in my disposition, behavior, and responses to life in. Jesus' name Amen.

Gifts Designed By God

As we prepare to close this chapter, I want to emphasize how important we are as women. **James 1:17 states,** *"Every good gift and every perfect gift is from above, and cometh down from the Father of lights, with whom is no variableness, neither shadow of turning."* When God presented Adam with his gift of Eve, she

You are an amazing GIFT designed by God!!

was the personification of perfection, beauty, sexiness, and ingenuity. Adam was so astonished at being bestowed with such an undeserved gift that he turned and called her,

"Woman," which I imagine he pronounced as (WHOA-MAN!!).

As descendants of this woman, who was later named Eve, we should never short change our importance by succumbing to negative perceptions of ourselves. Women we MATTER. We matter to God and our existence brings harmony and balance to the functionality of our world. I think we would all agree that our world is crazy, but without us, it would be thoroughly chaotic.

As gifts designed by the finger of God's love, we must understand that our DNA has been divinely coded with gifting reproductive capabilities. Many times, we feel that we are pulled in so many directions in life that staying afloat appears to be impossible. However, the amazing truth is that we never crumble, but we inevitably emerge energized with the willpower to strive forward. How can this be possible? It is because women have been coded to not only survive but to thrive and to achieve the impossible through the power of God.

What is gift? A gift defined is something bestowed voluntarily and without compensation upon an individual. God has voluntarily bestowed upon women the ability to gift companionship to a man through marriage, to gift eternal love to a child through motherhood, to gift the Kingdom of God with anointing and talent through ministry. In the forthcoming chapters of this book we will discuss each of these gifting abilities individually.

Chapter 2

The Gift of Motherhood

Scripture Foundation
II Timothy 1:5 (NLT)

"When I call to remembrance the unfeigned faith that is in thee, which dwelt first in thy grandmother Lois, and thy mother Eunice; and I am persuaded that in thee also."

I think one of the most beautiful gifts that God has given to women is the ability to become mothers. Whether through natural conception, adoption, or operating as a surrogate, the role of motherhood is priceless. It is filled with multifaceted experiences. It can be both a rewarding and thankless experience simultaneously. It can be overwhelming at one moment, and the next moment it can be filled with a sense of completeness and tranquility, as you relish in

Mom, are you taking care of YOURSELF?

your ability to adequately provide for the needs and happiness of your children.

Motherhood can be filled with immense moments of beaming pride at a child's accomplishment's and then filled with moments of sheer disgrace and shame at the same child's folly. Regardless of all of these mixed emotions, I think the average Godly mother would describe the role of motherhood as a blessing. Being entrusted by God to mold and shape a life is an amazing yet terrifying experience.

As moms we want the best for our children. We strive to provide them with the latest and best of everything from electronic devices to educational and social opportunities. We will work tirelessly to see these gems, which we refer to as our children, live comfortably.

However, in the process, oft-times we neglect our own needs. As mothers, it is our responsibility to keep ourselves healthy *mentally, physically, and socially* so that we can function at optimum level for our children.

Our Physical Health

Mom, you are amazing when it comes to taking little "Jack and Jill" to get their monthly, bi-monthly and annual checkups. However, when was the last time that you had an annual physical, mammogram, colonoscopy, Pap smear, dental or vision appointment? Many of us feel like we don't have time to take care of ourselves because we are inundated by the needs of our family.

However, our ability to care for our children will be hampered if we are not healthy.

I Corinthians 6:19-20 teaches us that our bodies are the temple of the Holy Spirit. Therefore we are required by God to take the best possible care of our bodies. This means that we should endeavor to keep our recommended checkups, do our monthly at home breast examinations, take our vitamins, and take our prescribed medication to control blood pressure, diabetes, cholesterol, or whatever else is necessary for our bodies to function properly. Likewise, we should commit to eating a healthy diet and exercising regularly.

The Holy Spirit began to deal with me regarding my health one day while I was sitting at my desk at work. He reminded me that I had not had an annual physical or pap smear in over a year. Likewise, I had passed the age of 40 and continued to procrastinate concerning scheduling my first mammogram, as I was not looking forward to it. The Lord instructed me to take care of myself so that I could be healthy and strong enough to take care of my son, Emmanuel. Since that time, I have had my recommended annual check-ups.

Have you been neglecting your health? The time to start the journey to a healthier you should begin

TODAY. Please do not wait until a serious condition develops that could have been avoided, if you would have maintained a healthier life style, to start taking better care of yourself. Your children and the world need you to be as healthy as possible so that you can make the godly impact in life that you were ordained to make. I urge you to consult your primary care physician today to discuss the status of your health!

Our Mental Health

Our children, regardless of their life stage, all possess an uncanny ability to stretch our tolerance and patience levels to our limits. Once our limits are surpassed, we live on the verge of "snapping" at any point. Mom, isn't it amazing that the average infant's first word is "da-da?" However, by the time they have matured into a toddler, their favorite word has transformed into "mama, mommy, ma, or mom!" For example, the child could have an awesome father, who happens to be sitting right next to them on the living room couch, but his or her first inclination is to cry out "Mommy!" when a need or desire arises in them. There have been times that I have coached my son to say the word "daddy." It worked for about a minute and then he reverted right back to crying out for "mommy."

Fulfilling the physical, emotional, social, and psychological needs of our children can become overwhelming. If we fail to ensure proper balance in our lives, and to maintain a realistic life perspective, we will quickly become burnt out. Many times the source of our absentmindedness is sheer exhaustion. Caring for our children can occupy so much of our thoughts that we can't remember simple things, such as where we placed our keys or our pocket book, so we find ourselves constantly scrambling to maintain order in our lives. When our "brain" begins to feel as if it's going to explode as of result of us having so much going on, it is a good indication that it is time for us to sit down, rest, and put everything on hold.

Psalms 23:2 states, *"He makes me to lie down in green pastures."* Dr. Charles L. Allen wrote a wonderful book entitled, "God's Psychiatry." In it he offers a superb interpretation of this verse. He teaches that God will allow us to become depleted of energy to the point that we are unable to function properly in an effort to alert us of the fact that we need to relax and allow our minds and bodies to rest and recuperate. God is so intelligent that He knows that our human tendency is to argue, "*I don't have time to rest.*" Therefore, at times, He has to MAKE us lie down by allowing us to become burned-out.

As mothers we have to learn to rest our brains. When our minds are at peace, we won't yell at our children as much, lose our tempers, or become so easily agitated. Instead of allowing our minds to shift into overload, we have to train our minds to stay on the Lord. Isaiah 26:3 states, "*Thou wilt keep him in perfect peace, whose mind is stayed on thee; because he trusteth in thee.*" Mom, take note to what the requirements are to enjoy peace of mind. The requirements are:

✓ Keep our mind on God

✓ Trust in God

Instead of stressing out about the needs of our children, we have to learn how to put their overall care in God's capable hands. God knows that our children have needs and wants, and He will provide for them through us if we are operating in obedience to His Word.

Mom, I encourage you to give yourself a good "time-out." I have quickly learned that children are resilient and will overcome certain disappointments quickly, such as not making it to a play date because mommy is tired and wants to rest. I've also learned that godly grandmothers, grandfathers, aunts, and uncles make wonderful babysitters! When you begin to feel like you need a break...remember they are just a text, phone call, or Facebook instant message away!

Our Social Well-Being

Mom, we need a social life independent of our children. Some of us spend so much time in children's activities that we have forgotten how to have fun in the company of other adults! Maintaining healthy and godly friendships enable us to maintain a sense of balance. Spending time in the company of good friend also helps us to:

- ✓ Maintain healthy life perspectives and remain relevant

- ✓ Maintain physical, mental and emotional health

Proverbs 27:17 states: *"As iron sharpens iron, so a friend sharpens a friend."*

Good friends usually spend a lot of time laughing together! **Proverbs 17:22(A) teaches us,** *"A cheerful heart is good medicine."* There is nothing like spending time with girl friends to chase away the blues. Some of our physical challenges would dissipate if we would simply enjoy life more!

Many studies have been conducted concerning the inter connection of our emotional and physical health. Dr. Charles Goodstein, New York University School of Medicine professor, as reported on www.everydayhealth.com, stated that: *"Thoughts and feelings as they are generated within the mind [can influence] the outpouring of hormones from* **the endocrine system, which in effect control much of what goes on within the body."[i]**

From this research and similar articles that I have read, it is my belief that some of us don't need medicine. We just need a good dose of fun, fellowship, and relaxation.

My girlfriends and I do our best to schedule a social outing every few months. Generally, we take turns spearheading an outing, whether it's to see a Broadway show, live game show, Gospel conference or concert or simply dining out. I find these gatherings to be extremely therapeutic. After an evening of fun and fellowship, I am revived and energized to resume my motherly duties with joy.

Sometimes our reluctance to participate in social outings is due to financial constraints. However, there is an abundance of opportunities to bond with friends socially at a low cost or for free. Examples of such are as follows:

- ✓ Promotional websites such as Groupon and Living Social that offer affordable fun activities
- ✓ Free events such as festivals and concert in the park, and movie night that are offered by various towns and municipalities throughout the year
- ✓ Free or low-cost events at local recreation centers, such as YMCA or town libraries
- ✓ Church sponsored activities, such as retreats, picnics, or fellowship brunches.

How would you rate your social life? Does it need a makeover? Perhaps the time has come for you to spend more time enjoying life. I encourage you to plan time to have fun and to relax.

A Mother's Gift of Prayer

I mentioned earlier that as mothers we want to afford our children the best of everything. I've quickly learned that one of the best gifts that we can invest in for our children is prayer. As Christian women, it is vital that we shield our children from the enemy's

Mom PRAY for your children daily!

attack through effective, consistent fervent prayer **(see James 5:16).**

Why should we pray? Prayer sensitizes our discernment and spirituality which enables us to recognize when our children are just being "kids" or when the enemy is influencing their behavior. The Holy Spirit will alert our spirit to know when it's time to shift into warfare mode for our children's behavior, disposition, emotional and mental stability. Sometimes the root of our children's poor behavior is demonic interference. As mothers, we have to know how to interrupt that interference through the power of prayer.

Why should we strive to be praying mothers? Prayer enables us to safeguard our children's future.

Part of our responsibility as mothers is to spend time with our children and *instruct them* about the realities of life. One of life's realities is that generational curses are real. As mothers, we need to be keenly aware of negative generational habits and behaviors that threaten to sabotage our children's productivity as a result of what "runs in our family." Sexual perversion, molestation, alcoholism, abuse, drug addiction, financial debt, lying, cheating, mental illness, spiritual depravity, and all manners of ungodliness can be inherited. As women of prayer, we have the right and authority to forbid these curses from overtaking the lives of our children. **Matthew 18:18 states:** *"I tell you the truth, whatever you forbid on earth will be forbidden in heaven, and whatever you permit on earth will be permitted in heaven."*

On the same token, based on this same scripture, we possess the right and power to permit good health, mental and financial stability, career and educational success and holy living in our children's lives.

Prayer for our children should not begin when we witness behaviors in our children that we don't like. Prayer for our children should begin from the womb and continue daily throughout our children's lives.

As soon as I found out that I was pregnant, I began praying for my son. I prayed throughout his formation in my womb. Likewise, even now as a toddler, I feel led by the Spirit to go into his room and pray for him as he sleeps in bed. I bind up generational curses, naming those that I am aware of that run in his father's blood line as well as in mine. I speak the blessings and favor of God over his life in faith. I speak into existence that he will accept Christ as Lord and Savior at a young age and be filled with the Holy Spirit. I rebuke the traps that the enemy has set for his demise and I pray success and prosperity over his life constantly. Though he is only a toddler, I believe that God will honor my prayers, and that I will see the fruit of my labor as he matures.

Since my son's birth, I have had countless people tell me that he is a prophet of God. As Mary did Jesus, I ponder each proclamation of his greatness in the kingdom of God in my heart **(see Luke 2:19)**. I already know that the enemy is going to fight the Word that has been spoken into my son's life, therefore I labor for him in prayer that the Word of God would prevail and the offense of the enemy would be weakened and deemed futile in his life.

Perhaps you have been giving your child(ren) everything except the gift of prayer. Why not add "pray for my children" on your daily to do list? Let's practice by pausing to pray now:

Let Us Selah and Pray
(Personalize the prayer by filling in the blanks)

"Father God, in the name of Jesus Christ, I thank You and I praise You for choosing me above all of the women upon the earth to birth (add your children's names_____). I dedicate my children to you and I trust you to meet all of their needs according to Philippians 4:19. Lord, teach me how to remain calm as a mother and to not operate in a spirit of anxiety. Your Word teaches that I am to be anxious (worried) about absolutely nothing, but I am to pray about everything and give You thanks for what You have already done based on Philippians 4:6. Lord, I realize this includes the well-being and the care of my children, so I place them in your hands. Please help me to not be impatient, or speak harshly to my children.

Lord, You said in Your Word that all souls belong to you. I claim that all my children will accept You into their hearts as Lord and Savior. I claim their holiness and commitment to You. You said in Your Word whatsoever I bind on earth You will bind in heaven and whatsoever I loose on earth, You will loosed in heaven (Matt 18:18) . Lord, I stand on Your Word and I bind in the name of Jesus every generational curse such as debt, sexual impurity, spiritual depravity, and depression._____ (pray them here) that wants to attach itself to my children. I speak that they will not have power over their lives and they will not be enslaved by them. Lord, I loose your peace, blessings, favor, protection, and strength over their lives. I pray in Your name that they will lack nothing but will live in the fullness of Your divine provision all of the days of their lives.

Lord, teach me how to take care of myself so that I am strong and well enough to take care of my children. Please forgive me for where I've neglected my physical, emotional, mental, and social health. Please help me to embrace your desire for me to be prosperous and to be in good health even as my soul prosperous. (3 John 1:2)

Lord, Jesus, I don't have all the answers to the questions and concerns that pertain to my children. However, I know that you do, so I willingly place them into your care.

Please give me wisdom to raise my children. I trust your leadership and expect to see great things transpire in the lives of my children. In Jesus' name, amen."

Chapter 3

The Gift of Marriage

Scripture Foundation
Hebrews 13:4 (NLT)

"Give honor to marriage, and remain faithful to one another in marriage. God will surely judge people who are immoral and those who commit adultery."

Marriage Defined

Truthfully speaking, I was quite reluctant to write this book due to my short tenure as a wife and as a mother. My rationale was that a more experienced voice would be required in order to author the subjects of marriage and motherhood. However, the Lord explicitly spoke into my spirit that if I shared the wisdom that I have gained thus far, it would be a blessing in the lives of many women.

Before divulging on the subject to marriage, I find it necessary to pause and define what a godly marriage is due to the times in which we are residing. Based on **Genesis 2:21-25,** marriage is a life-long covenant relationship, which exists between a man and a woman. This segment that I have penned discusses the relationship and role of a woman who is married to or desires to be married to a man.

Living out The Vows

The Reality of Marriage

In my four years of marriage, I have quickly learned that it is far easier to recite the marriage vows on the wedding day, than it is to live them out on a daily basis. To live out the vows with sincerity, and not solely out of

> **Marriage is a blessing but it is not a fairy tale!**

obligation, requires much patience, prayer, unconditional love, selflessness, forgiveness, maturity, more patience, more prayer, and more unconditional love, and more selflessness. I am not an advocate of describing marriage as being hard because:

1. ***Proverbs 18: 21 states,*** *"Death and life are in the power of the tongue: and they that love it shall eat the fruit thereof."* If we release into the atmosphere that our marriage is HARD, then our marriage will be HARD. However, should the state of our marriage be functioning below optimum desire, we have to decree prophetically that it is blessed in the name of Jesus until it improves.

2. Referring to the state of marriage as being HARD can serve as a deterrent to single people from getting married. After all, who wants to willfully enter into a life-long spiritually, emotionally, and financially binding union of HARDSHIP?

Rather, I choose to refer to the reality that marriage has challenges that require commitment and perseverance to overcome. Accepting the role of being a godly wife is not for the faint at heart, but it is for the woman who is determined to allow Christ to be seen in her at all times through the eyes of her husband.

Understanding the Marriage Vows

What are the marriage vows? The marriage vows serve as a verbal contract of commitment, love, fidelity, faithfulness and partnership that is made between a man and woman. They are solemn and sacred promises that we make to each other before God, an ordained minister, and oft times our loved ones. It is my belief that the vows are usually recited with sincerity, and that the couple genuinely desires to remain true to them. However, once the "honeymoon" phase of the marriage

Did you mean what you said at the altar??

ends, the aura of living happily ever after can slowly begin to fade. Is it possible that the vows were quoted with fairytale-like imagery filling our imaginations without our hearts fully comprehending what we were committing, too? Did we really mean it when we promised each other that we would stay together and only death itself could separate us? Hmm, I wonder did we really ponder the depth of this commitment prior to making it.

It is my persuasion that an in-depth study and dialogue of the marriage vows be conducing during premarital counselling. Couples need to be challenged regarding their understanding of the vows and the stamina required to maintain them. Let's take a didactic view of the traditional Christian marriage vows found in The Book of Common Prayers (1662).

Listed below are the 13 promises that husbands and wives make to one another on their wedding day when reciting these traditional vows:

1. To live **together** after God's ordinance in the holy estate of Matrimony
2. To love, comfort, honor one another
3. To keep in sickness

4. To keep in health;

5. Forsaking all others and keep to each other only as long as both shall live

6. To have and to hold from the wedding day forward regardless of:

   a) good times

   b) bad times

   c) seasons of prosperity

   d) seasons of lack

   e) seasons of sickness

   f) seasons of health

7. To love and to cherish, till death us do part, according to God's holy ordinance; and thereto I plight thee my troth.

We essentially recite these vows to one another blindly, as we have absolutely no idea what will transpire in our future that will challenge our dedication to each other. What happens should bad times arrive in our marriage? Let's view some examples below:

Example A (vows 1, 2, 5, and 6)

One of our bad times could very well be us falling out of love with our spouse or vice versa. Perhaps boredom has set into the relationship, loss of attraction, or an overall disinterest in each other. What do we do? Do we separate or seek a divorce?

What caused you to initially fall in love with your husband?

No, that is the incorrect response because we've pledged to stay together regardless of life's unpredictability. Do we get another boyfriend on the side who will bring more interest and excitement into our lives? Absolutely not because that would violate promise number 5 listed above. Do we just ignore each other and live as roommates? No, that's an unacceptable answer because our second and sixth promise to each other was to love, comfort, honor, and hold one another. What then should we do? As godly, women the answer is to do whatever it takes to fall back into love with our husbands. Should the reverse have occurred, where the husband has fallen out of love with us, we have to do whatever it takes for him to fall back into love with us. How do we do that?

Perhaps it will require us to apply the advice given to the Church of Ephesus by Jesus. The Church at Ephesus in **Revelations 2:5** were guilty of falling out of love with Him so He urged them to remember how things used to be between them and to revert back to doing the things that caused them to initially fall in love with Him.

It is very easy to become so common with each other after we have settled into marriage that we allow the passion, joy, and laughter to die in the relationship. Married couples should continue to date each other after the wedding. If attending movies, going to the beach, snow-boarding, horseback riding, mini-golf, dinner, etc. is what you did to enjoy time with each other prior to marriage, why does it have to stop COMPLETELY after marriage? Things obviously change due to increased financial responsibility or the bearing of children, but we have to strive to maintain enjoyable socialization with each other.

Perhaps we or our spouse have "let ourselves go" after getting married and/or bearing children. Weight gain has set in, and perhaps we do not have the time or energy to make trips to the hair salon, etc. Women, men are visual creatures and are driven by what they see. King David is a prime example of this truth. **II Samuel 11:2** records how King David saw a woman washing herself on the rooftop and he found her to be very beautiful. David became entrapped by not allowing his eyes to be submitted to the order of God! He should have looked away, but instead, he continued to gaze on Bathsheba until he eventually ended up in the bed with her and committed adultery, which eventually led to the murder of her husband. By no means am I defending David's actions. He was wrong and subsequently had to reap the consequences of his sin. I am merely supporting my point that men have a tendency to be moved by what they see.

We have to do our best to remain attractive to our husbands. Maintaining a comfortable weight and appearance gives the enemy less room to tempt our husband with other women, or falling into other forms of sexual impurity, such as pornography. We must be mature enough to accept our husband's constructive criticism regarding our appearance. His opinion of us should matter to us. I do not make this statement to give license to our husbands to control us or suffocate our individuality. However, we do have to consider what our husbands find as attractive and unattractive.

For example, I decided to strip my hair of chemical processes and opted to keep it in its natural state. I chose to wear twists because it was relatively easy to maintain and lasted for quite a while. I liked the hairstyle, but my husband absolutely positively hated it. He voiced his opinion to me every time I would wash my hair and restyle it with twists. At the time, I could have cared less that he felt that way because I needed something manageable. However, the last time my husband, complained the Holy Spirit convicted me. He alerted me to the fact that underneath my husband's complaints was the reality that he did not find me attractive with twisted hair. Since that time, I have learned how to maintain a manageable natural blow-out hairstyle that my husband loves. As soon as I changed it, I started to receive compliments from him that I had not heard from him in months. Wives, we have to remember that the things that attracted our spouses to us prior to marriage are the things that we should endeavor to maintain after marriage to preserve the attraction.

On the same token, our husbands need to remain attractive to us as well. If we no longer find them attractive due to weight gain, or lack of personal hygiene etc., then we should pray that God open up the door for us to be able to discuss it with them openly and honestly. Sometimes, in dealing with husbands, we have to enter in warfare prayer in order for a change to set in. We will discuss the gift of prayer in marriage later on.

If, God forbid, promise 5, *"Forsaking all others and keep to each other only as long as both shall live,"* is violated by one of the spouses, it is going to take in-depth forgiveness, prayer, and professional counselling to mend the relationship. Adultery does not mean that the marriage has to end, but it does mean that healing is required and a conscious effort on both the part of the wife and the husband has to be made in order to move past it.

Example B (vows 3, 6A and 6B)

Vows 3 and 4 detail our vow to remain committed and faithful to our spouse regardless of his health conditions. This means that, God forbid, our strapping, muscular, well-toned and able-bodied husband's health deteriorates our response and attitude towards him will not wane should his appearance change as a result of the illness. Likewise, we are also committing to assuming the financial responsibilities and inconvenience that we may incur as a result of our spouses illness without ever holding it against him. **Are you committed to your spouse in sickness?** Sickness and disease are a part of life and we do not know if it will occur, its formation or its severity. Taking a vow to remain faithful, loving, and kind to a spouse during seasons of affliction is a weighty promise. It would be wise for men and women to carefully consider the enormity of this commitment prior to marrying each other.

I personally know of three couples in which one of the spouses have been afflicted with debilitating diseases. One of the couples, the wife is sick, and the other two couples, the husbands are sick. All three healthy spouses have had to make life changing alterations as a result of accommodating their spouses. I'm amazed at the commitment of the healthy spouse because I have not seen them treat their partner negatively due to the illness.

I've personally been reminded of my vow to keep my husband in sickness and in health a few times when he fell ill. Prior to God rebuking me, I would inwardly complain, because I had to take off of work to care for him and I was annoyed at the inconvenience of it all. The last instance in which my husband needed me is when I received the rebuke from the Lord. The Lord clearly reminded me that I promised to care for my husband in sickness and health. The Lord instructed me to stop complaining and tend to my husband's need with gentleness and kindness.

Handling the difficult times in marriage requires a MATURE approach

Caring for a sick spouse is not easy. It requires patience, endurance, and prayer. It may even require professional counselling or assistance from a support group when times are tough. If you are struggling with adjusting to caring for your ill husband, I encourage you to remember the vow that you made to him and to seek God through prayer for His strength to aid you. Likewise, seek out support from your church or a Christian counselling center that can offer you guidance in navigating through this area of life. I advise dating couples to have an open an in-depth conversation regarding pre-existing health conditions prior to committing to marriage.

In promises 6A and 6b listed above, we promise each other to stick it out during good times and bad times. It is easy for us to be loving, kind, and generous to each other when all of the bills are paid, our savings account is overflowing, and we are getting along with each other wonderfully. These good times in marriage should be celebrated and cherished. However, the reality is that bad times do arrive in our lives periodically. Finances may be sparse, which can cause tremendous amounts of stress on the relationship. Likewise, wives and husbands do not always agree, and at times will simply get on each other's last nerves. I will take it a step further and say that there are days that we simply do not like each other. There are even times when we do not feel the same depth of love and attraction for our husbands that we did when we first married them. I would classify these times as bad times that require a mature approach and outlook.

A mature approach to handling these bad times is to remember that our husbands are God's children and we have to treat and speak to them with the utmost respect, love, gentleness, and kindness. When things are going wrong, the answer is not to shut down communication, argue, become belligerent, or turn against our husbands. The bad times requires a wife who is ready to pray consistently and fervently until the bad times get better. She must pray honestly and openly about how she feels and pray for God's blessings on her husband. It is not always easy to pray when things are difficult, but it is doable with the help of the Holy Spirit.

The bad times can stretch the depth of our commitment to each other to its limit. Wife, if you feel as if your bad times outweigh your good times in your marriage, it's time to pray and ask God to give you a clear and precise strategies to rescue your marriage from pending destruction. Prayer works. When I stopped arguing with my husband and began to pray....God began to change things. We will discuss the gift of prayer in marriage in more details later on.

The last two points under promise 6 that I want to address, our vows to remain committed to the relationship for richer or poorer. Based on this, it is not a good idea for couples to marry for money or for what the potential husband possesses. The reality is that anything can happen that can cause us to lose our possessions....just ask the biblical character Job. He was the richest man on earth and literally lost everything overnight! Apparently, his wife was unprepared for the devastation that hit her family and desired to renege on her commitment to Job by encouraging him to commit suicide **(see Job 1 and 2).**

Wives, it is possible for joblessness, stock market crashes, grand larceny, fraud, identity theft or a host of other maladies to occur that can alter our financial comfort. When we are committed to our marriage, we will have to work through the tough financial times together.

We should strive to be financially responsible. Meaning that neither the husband nor wife should be the cause of financial stress due to mismanagement, or selfishness with contributing to the household income. Selfishness and irresponsibility places unnecessary stress and strain on the marital relationship.

When we decide to marry, then we have also decided to have a shared wallet. Allocation of the household finances should be agreed upon between the spouses. Financial selfishness in a marriage is a great way to destroy the marriage. Marriage means that your husband's money belongs to you and your money belongs to your husband.

Vow 7

The last vow that I want to bring attention to is number 7 which states, *"To love and to cherish, till death us do part, according to God's holy ordinance; and thereto I plight thee my troth."* Wives, if we love, and cherish our husbands, we will not belittle them, speak disrespectfully to them, call them derogatory names, withhold our bodies from them sexually, or be

What does love got to do with it?? It has EVERYHING to do with it!!

physically, emotionally, or mentally abusive to them. Love does not respond in an ill-manner. **I Corinthians 13** beautifully describes what love is: *"Love is patient and kind. Love is not jealous or boastful or proud[5] or rude. It does not demand its own way. It is not irritable, and it keeps no record of being wronged.[6] It does not rejoice about injustice* *but rejoices whenever the truth wins out.* [7] *Love never gives up, never loses faith, is always hopeful, and endures through every circumstance." (NLT)*

Wives, it is not always easy to show love to our husbands, especially if we feel as if they are not showing love to us. However, I'm learning that when we display love because we want to please and honor God, it makes it easy to do. Sometimes, based on our husband's response toward us, we may feel as if they don't deserve our forgiveness or kindheartedness. I have felt that way at times in my marriage. However, God reminded me that if I didn't forgive my husband, then I couldn't receive forgiveness from God. Likewise, He reminded me of all the kind things He does for me on a daily basis, such as providing all of my needs that I don't deserve, but He does it anyway.

When we find it difficult to show love towards our husbands we have to make it a matter of prayer. If we ask God to show us how to love our husbands, and to open up the right opportunity for us to discuss the issue with our husbands, God will do it.

Perhaps you are a wife who is being mistreated instead of being shown godly love from your spouse. I urge you to not only make it a matter of prayer, but to seek godly and professional counseling. I do not believe that it is the will of God for anyone to suffer abuse. If you are experiencing emotional, sexual, or physical abuse from your husband, it is time to seek help now.

In conclusion of our discussion of the vows, I encourage wives everywhere to be mindful of what is written in **Ecclesiastes 5:5:** *"Better is it that thou shouldest not vow, than that thou shouldest vow and not pay."*

Likewise, I encourage engaged women, and single women who desire to marry, to carefully consider the vows prior to making them. Make sure that you love the man that you intend to marry enough to keep ALL of the vows.

Wives, at times our pride surfaces and causes us to want to renege on one or more of our vows. However, I believe that each wife who is reading this book desires to please God in her marriage. If we condition our minds toward honoring God, we will truly emerge as the **Proverbs 31:11,** *"...whose husband knows he can trust her and will greatly enrich his life."*

Help Meet What?

Have you ever experienced feeling as if you do more than your fair share in your marriage? Perhaps you contribute a reasonable or substantial amount of money to the household income, manage most of the household chores, plan most of the family vacations and recreational activities, do the majority of the grocery shopping, primarily oversee the day-to- day needs of the child(ren), and spend the most times in prayer in comparison to your spouse. You may ponder why it seems that the responsibilities shared between husbands and wives appear so incredibly lopsided and unbalanced. Lord knows I have. Please do not misunderstand me, I have a very good husband; however, there have been instances where I scratched my head regarding the seemingly disproportionate expectations.

In the infancy stage of marriage, I used to complain and be resentful because I felt that I was being taken advantage of. I called myself "telling God" on my husband in prayer. One day the Lord challenged my complaints by having me to read **Genesis 2:18** which describe His intention for creating wives. The scripture reads in the KJV: *"And the LORD God said, It is not good that the man should be alone; I will make him an **help meet** for him."*

The Lord said to me that, *"I made you to HELP him. I left it open-ended and I did not put stipulations on the extent or limit to which you are to help your husband."* Wow! I was not expecting God to say that to me! What an eye-opener this was. I had never considered the depth of the responsibilities of being a help meet. To be honest with you, during my single years, my expectation was that my husband would be the primary provider of all my needs. In retrospect, I realize that my expectation was misplaced because, first of all, the Apostle Paul specifically said in ***Philippians 4:19 (KJV): "****But **my God shall supply** all your need according to his riches in glory by Christ Jesus."*

I never, ever should have expected my husband to meet any of my needs. Yes, he should provide as the head of the household, but I was to assist as needed. Secondly, the WOMAN is the one, according to the Scripture, who is called to assist the husband! The husband's job is to love his wife unconditionally to the point that he would be willing to risk his life for her **(Ephesians 5:25).**

Wives, wherever our husbands may be experiencing a deficit, it is part of our responsibility to help him to succeed, and we are not to hold our contribution against him. For example, if God has blessed us women to have a higher income than our husbands, we should never ever throw it in his face! We should be ecstatic that God has entrusted us to help our husbands to live comfortably through the level of finances that He has allowed our hands to produce. **Proverbs 31:11** confirms this truth. It states:

Strive to become the Proverbs 31 Wife!

"The heart of her husband doth safely trust in her, so that he shall have no need of spoil."

Proverbs 31 provides a clear and concise description of a wife whose husband views her character as impeccable, self-sacrificing, supportive, upright and overall honorable. I encourage all women to read the text in its entirety in the New Living Translation as it is easily readable and understandable. A synopsis of this woman's character is below as described in the text:

✓ She is not lax in any area of life. She puts her foot forward in all that she does.

✓ She multitasks. She successfully manages her household while she simultaneously works outside of the home.

✓ She makes home cooked meals for her family. She saves money by making clothing for herself and her household.

✓ She ensures that her family's future is secure by ensuring that they have what they need ahead of time based on the seasons.

✓ She uses her talents to help her husband financially by selling and marketing her wool and linen products that she makes by hand.

✓ She knows how to invest her money. She looks for profitable business opportunities such as buying fields and uses the profits to plant vineyards to yield a tangible return on her investment.

✓ She is financially responsible. Her husband completely trusts her to have access to the family finances. He knows that she will not cause him to go into debt but will actually enrich his life.

✓ She keeps her appearance attractive to her husband by dressing in fabrics such as linen and colors, such as purple that appeal to him.

✓ She speaks life into her husband. Whenever she speaks to him, her words are saturated with wisdom.

This woman is the epitome of what it means to embrace the role of being a help meet. She is so passionate about caring for her husband and her children that her husband praises her, and her children proudly stands to bless her.

Sidebar: please note that I am in no way encouraging wives to settle for a lazy husband who does not work. That would be contradictory to the scripture which advises in *Philippians 3:9(B) NLT:* "*Those unwilling to work will not get to eat.*"

Husbands need to be willing to do whatever it takes to provide for their household. The point that I am attempting to make is that as wives, we should expect that our assistance will be needed. Also, I am not advocating nor issuing a license of laziness to our husbands. **I Peter 3:7** reminds husbands that wives are physically the weaker of the two and we should be treated with understanding. Husbands should understand that they should help around the house as our energy levels are limited. Wives, I am simply suggesting that we understand, that based on Proverbs 31, women have been doing "more than their fair share" for centuries, so it's not unusual for you to feel as if you are. Rest assured that God has created in us the unique ability to successfully multitask.

It is my prayer and desire to one day fully live up to the description of the Proverbs 31 wife. I believe that should be the goal of all godly women, and with the help of the Holy Spirit, we will achieve this goal.

A Wife's Gift of Prayer

Perhaps you have noticed the numerous times that I have referred to prayer thus far in the reading. My experiences over the course of the past few years have taught me the importance of "Selah and pray." Selah is a Hebrew word that refers to the need to stop and listen, or to pause. I am learning that when I

A wife's prayer is a powerful weapon!

stop and pause to pray, I make more intelligent and informed decisions. God has been allowing me to learn the art of "Selah and pray" as a mother, as a wife, as a minister, and as money maker. I only wish that I would have yielded to God earlier in life and sought Him for guidance more fervently. I would have made far less poor choices if I would have done so.

As wives, why should we pray for our husbands? I will answer that question with a series of questions:

- ✓ Has arguing and fighting with your husband worked for you?
- ✓ Has nagging your husband to do things motivated him into action?
- ✓ Has shutting down communication and refusing intimacy with your husband worked for you?
- ✓ Has flying off the handle in anger and retaliating against your husband worked for you?

✓ Has crying hysterically and pouring out your heart to him changed the situation?

More than likely, you have answered with an emphatic "no" to my queries. You may have experienced some victories using these methods, but I can imagine that they were short lived. The answer to seeing positive change and progress in the lives of our husbands and in the state of our marriage is to pray.

Commit to praying FOR your husband and not ABOUT Him!

It takes perseverance, discipline, dedication, and commitment to pray **FOR** a spouse and not **ABOUT** a spouse. There is a tremendous difference in each of these approaches. When we pray **FOR** our husbands, we ae seeking **GOD'S BEST** and **GOD'S intention** for his life REGARDLESS of what we want. When we pray ABOUT our spouse, we are essentially tattle-telling on our husbands to God. I will admit that I reigned as the "queen of tattle-telling" on my husband to God when we were first married. I will also admit that at times when I'm frustrated, I have found myself reverting back to being a tattle-teller. However, I've noticed that God usually doesn't respond to my expectations when I'm tattling. God indeed listens to me; however, His response back normally is to show me where I was wrong in the situation, or how I could have handled it differently. When I realized that the prayer strategy that I had been utilizing was not altering the climatic conditions of my marriage, I decided that the time had come to change my approach.

I began to pray and ask God to help me to understand why the situation was worsening and why He had not intervened in my situations. The Lord spoke to me very clearly and alerted me to the fact that my initial motives in prayer for my husband were simply wrong and misguided. Uh-Oh! There is that word "motive" mentioned again regarding my relationship with the Lord. The Lord let me know that my intention in praying for my husband was because I simply wanted him to comply with my terms and my perceived needs. I was not praying for my husband in order for him to become all that he was called to be in God, but for my own convenience. In a nutshell, I was praying selfish prayers that God would not answer.

I concluded that for the health of my marriage I had to stop praying ABOUT my husband and begin to sincerely pray FOR my husband. When I changed strategies, I began to see positive results. Let's look at an example below of a wife praying ABOUT her husband verses praying FOR her husband. Note that in both prayer scenarios listed below the situation remains the same.

Scenario 1: PRAYER ABOUT JOSH

"Dear Lord, please look on my husband, Josh. He is always complaining and speaking harshly to me. He is a negative person and I am tired of his mistreatment of me. His negativity is starting to rub off on me and I'm sick of it! Please show him that he is wrong to treat me the way that he does. Let him know that I'm a good wife and I deserve better. Jesus, I am not going to continue to put up with this. If you do not intervene and fix this situation, then I am going to start giving him a taste of his own medicine. I pray these things in faith in your name. Amen."

Scenario 2: PRAYER FOR JOSH

"Dear Lord, please remember my husband Josh and minister to him right now. Let him know that, God, you hear the negative words that he speaks, but you understand that it is just the manifestation of an area of his heart that he has not

submitted to you. Let him know that you have called him to be the head of this house and that he has the power to speak life, and not death, into our family and marriage according to your Word. Lord, let Josh know that if he submits all of his disappointments, hurts, and frustrations to you that you have the power to heal his heart. Once his heart is healed it will be easy for him to speak lovingly and kindly to me. Lord, his actions hurt me. However, I realize that the enemy is influencing his behavior. I acknowledge that there has been a breakdown in Josh's relationship with you that would cause him to speak harshly to me. Lord, help me to not retaliate. Strengthen me to win him over by my gentle, kind, loving, and godly conversation in accordance to your Word. Lord, I pray this in your name and I expect to see positive results. Amen."

Note the difference in the tones of the two prayers. In both instances Josh has been speaking negatively to Hannah. In the first scenario, Hannah's frustration is apparent and she makes the entire situation about her. Not one time in the first scenario does Hannah consider that the root cause of her husband's behavior be due to a breakdown in his relationship with Christ. Her heart is filled with hurt and anger as she prays. She is too offended to allow the Holy

Spirit to intercede through her on behalf of her husband according to **Romans 8:26.**

In the second scenario, Hannah acknowledges that she has been hurt by her husband's behavior. She also acknowledges that she will need the strength and help of God to not respond out of her emotions by retaliating against Josh. However, she realizes that she is just the recipient of a break down in his relationship with Christ. She does not focus on her pain, but she focuses on her husband's need to restore his communication with the Lord through confession of what is troubling him. Hannah recognizes that the enemy is behind it all. She understands that when Josh gets things right with God, he won't have a problem treating her right. The motive of Hannah's prayer is to see improvement in Josh's behavior towards her as a by-product of the improvement in his behavior towards God!

Let me reiterate that committing to praying FOR a husband as opposed to praying ABOUT a husband takes practice. I'm learning that in order for me to effectively pray for my husband I truly have to submit to the will of God. I cannot operate in pride, stubbornness, arrogance or disobedience. Effective prayer requires effective surrendrance to God's way of doing things.

It may take a while to see the manifestation, but I believe that in time, our husbands will appreciate our gift of prayers for them. I choose to believe that my prayers on behalf of my husband will help him to succeed in every aspect of life, which will catapult success in my own life. *James 5:16(B) states*, "*The effectual fervent prayer availeth much.*" (KJV). Prayer is not exclusive to specific situations. As long as faith is applied, and we pray in accordance to God's will, all things are subject to the power of prayer. Let's take a moment and "Selah and Pray" before we continue.

****Let Us Selah and Pray****

"*Father God in the name of Jesus Christ. It is me again_____ (insert your name). I am requesting your help in becoming the Proverbs 31 wife to my husband _____. Lord, I realize that the role of a wife is vitally important and that it involves many tasks and responsibilities. Sometimes I do not feel strong enough to live up to the expectations of my husband let alone Yours. However, I embrace Philippians 4:16, "That I can do all things through*

Christ which strengtheneth me." This includes becoming the **Proverbs 31** wife.

Lord, after reading **Proverbs 31,** I realize that my shortcomings as a wife are _____, _____, _____. Lord, please help me to do better. Please give me a strategy to overcome the areas of my life that I am currently operating below your expectations.

Lord, please help me to cherish and keep the vows that I made to my husband on my wedding day. I do not always feel like showing kindness, love, and respect to him. I do not always feel like sharing or sacrificing my desires in order to please him. Lord, when I am weak, please be my strength to do the right thing. I accept that Your grace is sufficient according to **2 Corinthians 12:9,** to bring us through every situation that arises in our marriage.

Lord, please help me to offer the gift of prayer to my husband. Please help me to push past how I feel and genuinely pray for my husband and not about him. I pray that my motives in prayer would be right and that I would allow your Spirit to pray through me for my husband.

Lord Jesus, please bring a refreshment and renewal into my marriage. Please teach me how to love and respect my husband. Please teach my husband how to love and to respect me. Help us to fall back in love with each other on a daily *basis. Lord Jesus, I commit my marriage into your hands and I believe that in your name we will successfully keep our vows to each other until death us do part, amen."*

To The Single Ladies in Waiting

Having been single until the age of 35, I have a soft spot in my heart for single Christian women who desire to be married. I am especially sensitive to those who may feel as if they have passed the "prime marrying age." I thought it would be fitting to allocate space in this book to encourage this genre of women. **Singles you are WORTH THE WAIT!!**

I write this section to the single women under the assumption that you have taken the time to thoroughly read the preceding pages on marriage. If you have not done so, I encourage you to do so as my writing perspective to you will refer to some of the points made in that section of the book. I strategically placed the singles discussion after the chapter on marriage because I wanted to offer you some things to consider prior to agreeing to marry your future mate. I desire for you to be prepared spiritually and emotionally. It is imperative that you understand some of the challenges that you may face during marriage.

Let me begin our conversation by affirming to all single women that your desire to be married is valid and based on Biblical principles. *Genesis 2:24 states, "Therefore shall a man leave his father and his mother, and shall **cleave** unto his wife: and they shall be one flesh."* This Scripture teaches us that the longing that you have to be connected to your male counterpart is a natural occurrence. When God extracted Adam's rib to create woman, **(Genesis 2:22), it** signified God's intention for man and woman to dwell together in unity according to His holy standards.

I believe that it is the will of God for you to be married, if that is your desire. However, my belief is rooted in you accepting the man that God has for you and not merely settling in a relationship for the sake of saying that you "have somebody." This is the worst thing that you can do and the end results will be a sea of regrets when you realize that you vowed your life to the wrong man. Single women, whatever you do, please refuse to "walk over a diamond to pick up a cubic zirconia" in terms of choosing your husband. This is a similar statement that I heard a preacher make many years ago when I was a teenager and it made a lasting impression upon my life. In order to fully absorb the wisdom of this statement, we must first understand the key differences that exist between natural diamonds and cubic zirconia.

There is a popular saying that states that, *"Diamonds are a girls' best friend."* Famed actress Marilyn Monroe sang the following lyrics:

> *"...But square-cut or pear shape,*
> *These rocks don't lose their shape*
> *Diamonds are a girl's best friend..."*

If I could afford them, I would own an innumerable assortment of these "best friends." For me, diamonds represent beauty, wealth, and prestige. These are qualities that I am attracted too. I believe that I am worth receiving a diamond, as do all of God's single daughters.

Refuse to walk over a Diamond to pick up a Cubic Zirconia... or worst yet... GLASS!!

Let's take a moment and rate our past and/or present relationships based on "diamond status." Would you classify the man that you were/are involved with as a diamond or a cubic zirconium? Is he the real thing or just a look-alike? Does he add value and beauty to your life or does he strip you of strength and your brilliance? Perhaps he is physically attractive and "sparkles" like a diamond, but when you do an honest appraisal of his character, you are having second thoughts. Is it possible that you may have walked over a true gem of a man because he was not the height, weight, skin tone, baritone, hair texture, or professional that you had envisioned yourself with? Have you instead picked up a cubic zirconium?

These are two thought provoking questions that I challenge you to answer. The commitment and responsibilities of marriage should not be taken lightly. You must be sure that you are making covenant with the real thing and not an imitation. How can we distinguish a diamond from a cubic zirconium? Let's examine it from a natural perspective.

Let's first establish that to the naked eye, both stones look alike. It takes a skilled professional with proper equipment to be able to distinguish between the two gems.

The most fascinating feature of the diamond, in my opinion, is the fact that these beautiful gems are a natural production of the earth dating back billions of years. They are highly durable and have a myriad of desirable qualities. Let's look at some of the attributes of natural diamonds and equate them to our relationships:

1. **Natural diamonds are man-made and take billions of years to form:**

Ask yourself this question, **is this relationship that you are in God-made or is it man-made?** Is this the husband that God ordained for you from the time that you were conceived in your mother's womb? When the relationship is God-made, it will exhibit similar qualities of the God-made diamond.

2. **Diamonds don't become cloudy in heated situations:**

Natural diamonds maintain their clarity and brilliance in heated situations. Cubic Zirconium, however, becomes cloudy and loses its brilliance. How does your potential spouse handle conflict, disagreements and challenges? Does he maintain his luster, composure, and brilliance as a diamond does when it is placed in "heated situations?" Or does he become angry, reclusive, aloof, depressed or difficult to deal with when things go wrong? Ask yourself, if he falls into the latter description, can you deal with that until *"DEATH DO THE TWO OF YOU PART,"* should you decide to marry him.

3. <u>**A true diamond not only beautifies but it adds value**</u>:

When appraised, a diamond can add financial gain to the owner's life. It is an asset. Likewise, a diamond can become a family heirloom that can be passed down from one generation to another. A cubic zirconium, on the other hand, though beautiful, does not have appraisal value and therefore will not provide prosperity to the owner's life. Let's consider these questions in comparison to the value of our relationship:

✓ Does your intended spouse ADD value to your life or does it appear that you are losing yourself spiritually, emotionally, mentally, or financially? Is the atmosphere of your relationship admirable to your children that they will want to replicate it in their marriages?

- ✓ If you marry your intended spouse, is it going to make your life better or worse? This should be thought about carefully. The old saying still reigns true, "I can do bad all by myself." Remember that when you marry, you assume your spouse's financial blessings or woes.
- ✓ Will you prosper emotionally, mentally, and spiritually if you marry this man? Or will you be drained and stripped of vigor and strength as a result of stress stemming from your marriage.

Ladies, I believe that God has someone special for you and I encourage you to wait on Him to divinely connect the two of you. I encourage you to allow God to speak to you about your future spouse. It very well could be the man that it is not your "type" and that you would never have considered as God's choice for you. He may not have been your first choice, but he is an absolute diamond and would love you as "Christ loved the church and gave himself for it." **(Ephesians 5:25 KJV).** Do not settle for cubic zirconium in your relationship. You are a diamond, and you deserve nothing less. Let's take a moment to "Selah and Pray."

Let Us Selah and Pray

"Lord, in the name of Jesus, please remember me and my desire for a husband. God, sometimes I get discouraged and wonder if marriage is for me. Deep in my heart, I know that the desire that I have for a husband was placed there by You, so I choose to trust You to divinely connect us to each other. Please help me not to give into impatience or desperation and end up settling for a cubic zirconium for a husband as opposed to a real diamond. Lord, just as you made natural diamonds, I choose to believe that you have made a diamond husband for me who will be in love with You and will also be in love with me. Please touch my spiritual eyes and my heart and help me to not walk over a diamond because he does not come in the "package" that I was looking for. Help me to recognize the godly qualities that you have placed in him and help me to know that You have chosen him for me. I thank You in advance for hearing my prayer and settling my spirit. In Jesus' name, amen."

Chapter 4

The Gift of Ministry

Ministry Defined

Most of the Christian women that I know sense a" higher call" from God to do something to help to advance His Kingdom. Some have tapped into the niche of service that Christ has called for them, while others are still seeking Him for clarity, wisdom and direction. This journey of discovery of walking in our purpose can be referred to as ministry.

Many in the Christian arena have a misconstrued perception of what ministry is. I think most of our thoughts initially gravitate to preachers who stand before massive congregations of people proclaiming the Gospel of Jesus Christ when we discuss the idea of ministry. This is indeed ministry, but there are many other arms or outlets of ministry that is the responsibility of all Christians. Regardless of whether we have an assembly appointed position, title or license, we are all called to minister, or to serve in the realm of delivering the message of Jesus Christ in one way or another. *Isaiah 43:10 (KJV) states,* "*Ye are my witnesses, saith the Lord, and my servant whom I have chosen: that ye may know and believe me, and understand that I am he: before me there was no God formed, neither shall there be after me."*

When we accept Christ as our Lord and Savior, we become witnesses of His redeeming power through our lifestyles. We become His ministers who are called to serve Him and to serve others for the upbuilding of His Kingdom. The definition of ministry in its most simplistic form simply means "to serve."

Who have we been called to minister to? We are called first and foremost to minister to God, and then we are called to minister to everyone that He allows us to come into contact with.

Ministering to God
Psalm 24:3-6

"Who may climb the mountain of the Lord? Who may stand in his holy place? Only those whose hands and hearts are pure, who do not worship idols and never tell lies. They will receive the Lord's blessing and have a right relationship with God their savior. Such people may seek you and worship in your presence, O God of Jacob". (NLT)

Our first priority in ministry is to ensure that we are genuinely serving the Lord. The church world is saturated with enough people operating in ministerial capacities while lacking a power infused relationship with the Lord. Christ desires to have an intimate relationship with us

How would you rate your ministry to the Lord?

and He extends the invitation to all who are willing to meet His eligibility requirements. His requirements are simplistic and straightforward as stated in the opening text of this section. He requires us to

1. Have clean hands, Have a pure heart,
2. Refrain from idol worship (which means we do not put anything or anyone before Him. Our allegiance is exclusively to Him),
3. To be a speaker and representative of the truth, and not a liar or a deceiver.

Those who possess these qualities are the true ministers and worshippers of Christ. They operate under His blessings and His righteousness

Ladies, if we are going to minister unto the Lord, then we have to adopt a lifestyle of sanctification. I grew up on the teaching of sanctification. Today, however, it is a much underused yet very much needed teaching in the church at large. Many of us want to experience the tangible presence of God and see the miracles wrought by His hands, but we have not submitted to a lifestyle of sanctification. Jesus knew that sanctification was a necessity so when he prayed for his disciples and He asked God to: *"Sanctify them through thy truth: thy word is truth."* **(John 17:17 KJV)**

Sanctification simply means to be set apart. We are called to be Holy as God is Holy **(see *Leviticus* 11:44).** Therefore we must be set apart from practices and environments that exhibit the opposite of holiness. It is not our style of apparel that constitutes holiness; rather the condition of our heart which is revealed through our lifestyle.

I find it necessary to interject and provide a lucid explanation of what does and does not constitute holiness according to biblical teaching. I grew up in an era in which many believers associated holiness and sanctification primarily with the length, color, style and fabrication of another person's outer garments. If a professing Christian appeared a certain way, he or she would be deemed "holy." However, for some odd reason, emphasis was not placed on the disposition and character of the individual. According to scripture, a sanctified lifestyle is based on character. The Apostle Paul provides a straightforward description of a lifestyle void of sanctification and holiness. According to **I Corinthians 6:9-11 9 (AMP)** and unsanctified lifestyle is characterized by:

- ✓ *sexual immorality,*
- ✓ *idolatry,*
- ✓ *effeminate by perversion,*
- ✓ *homosexuality,*
- ✓ *thievery*
- ✓ *greed,*
- ✓ *drunkenness,*
- ✓ *verbal abusers (those whose words are used as weapons to abuse, insult, humiliate, intimidate, or slander,*
- ✓ *swindlers*

Women, we must understand that sanctification is far more reaching than us refraining from physically engaging in these activities that do not please God, but is inclusive of us not supporting them through what we choose to allow ourselves to be entertained by through the media. For example, a few years ago I found myself addicted to the television series "Scandal," which is filled with murder, lust, adultery, homosexuality, deception and every type of behavior that opposes sanctification. Shortly after I began to follow the series, I was faced with a very challenging situation in my personal life. I was under a great deal of emotional stress, and honestly, in the process, I developed a thirst for revenge. Instead of fasting, and praying about my problem, I found myself considering some of the tactics that I had seen in the show for usage in my personal life. Thankfully, the Lord began to severely rebuke me for my foolish contemplations. My thoughts had become unsanctified because of what I had been watching on television. I repented, discontinued watching Scandal, and returned to my roots in fasting and prayer. Several months later, God intervened in my situation and worked things out for me.

Being sanctified, or set-apart, does not mean that we have to live a life of seclusion. It does, however, mean that we exclude those things from our life that will interfere with our relationship with the Lord.

How do we minister unto the Lord? We minister to the Lord through pure worship, prayer, praise and meditation. God desires to restore the intimate relationship with us that He once possessed with Adam, in the Garden of Eden, prior to the fall. He wants to meet with us in the "cool of the day, *(Genesis 3:8)*, but that can only be accomplished through committing to a life of sanctification.

Ladies, you have been called to be a minister to the Lord. You do not need a license, title, or platform in a church building. All you need is to worship the Lord in Spirit and in truth. When we worship God in Spirit and truth, we answer the call to the ministers that He is looking for *(see John 4:23-24)*.

Our family needs our spiritual strength, wisdom, and guidance!

Family Next

Our second audience to which we are called to minister to is our families.

Whether we are married, single, sisters, cousins, aunts, mothers or grandmothers, ministering Christ to our family members should be a top priority. *1 Timothy 5:8 (NLT) states*, *"But those who won't care for their relatives, especially those in their own household, have denied the true faith. Such people are worse than unbelievers."*

I believe this scripture not only applies to provision of the natural needs of our family, but to their spiritual needs as well. It's wonderful for us to make sure Christ is made known to the world through our preaching, teaching, pastoring, outreach & ministry. However, how sad is it if our own children, grandchildren, nieces and nephews, brothers, sisters, parents and cousins have either not heard about Christ, been taught the basic scriptures, or have been introduced to the foundations of salvation directly from us? Worst yet, if they have not SEEN the love of Christ shine through us to them.

The best witness for Christ that we can be to our family members is through our behavior and responses. If they hear us speak of Him and His teachings publicly but see us living in direct opposition of what we proclaim, we confuse them about the realness and the power of the Word of God.

Our offspring should want the God that we serve because they have seen His love and faith illuminate through us. Timothy, a young minister of the Gospel, was living proof of becoming a Christian as a result of the godly lifestyle that he witnessed from his mother and grandmother. The Apostle Paul encouraged Timothy with these words: *"I remember your genuine faith, for you share the faith that first filled your grandmother Lois and your mother, Eunice. And I know that same faith continues strong in you."* **(2 Timothy 1:5) NLT**

Ministering to our family members is probably the most challenging group of people to minister to. Our families tend to know us "without makeup," meaning they are more intimate with our flaws. Likewise, family members have the ability to taunt and to push our patience and tolerance levels to our maximum limit.

When we generally have a heart to see our family members soar in Christ, we should not be surprised when we begin to experience conflict, confrontation, and misunderstanding begin to arise between us. The enemy will do whatever he can to tarnish our godly influence with our family members as a means for them to reject Christ. We must be aware of his strategic interference and commit to maintaining a spirit of forgiveness among our family members so that our testimony of Christ is not jeopardized. This will require prayer and determination as it will require many times for us to have to accept the blame when we are innocent and to apologize even when we have done nothing wrong.

It is our responsibility to educate our family about salvation. We should not expect the church to have a greater spiritual influence on our family members than what we do. Mothers with young children must commit to allocating time to spend teaching their children the Word of God and the principles of prayer. We cannot rely on our local church's Sunday school or youth department to assume this responsibility.

In addition to ministering to the spiritual needs of our family, we have to be committed to ministering to their natural need for our time and our attention. Fellow pastors, evangelists, missionaries, and ministers, we must spend adequate time with our spouses and our children just having fun and enjoying life. We do not want our children or our spouses to resent God because we spent so much time "doing ministry" that we miss events that are held to celebrate our families' achievements, accomplishments, or passions. We have to commit to maintaining a balanced lifestyle.

More Than a Paycheck

Have you ever considered that perhaps God strategically allowed you to beat out all of the other candidates who were interviewing for your job **Can your co-workers see Christ in YOU??** position because of a spiritual need in one of your fellow coworkers? Perhaps there is someone there that needs your prayers, support, encouragement, discipleship or witness of Jesus Christ. Perhaps you have been placed there for a reason far greater than receiving a paycheck.

I must admit that during my 20+ years working on the corporate side of the retail industry that my main focus was career and financial advancement. My priority was not to be a blessing to souls on my job but to climb the corporate ladder of success. Please do not misunderstand me, I have always made it known that I was a Christian and I would take advantage of the opportunity to share Christ with my coworkers whenever possible. However, it was not until my most recent position that I really became aware of God's strategic ministerial tactics. I have learned that when God strategically places you in a position to strengthen someone else in the faith, the enemy will do all that he can to sabotage God's plan.

When I was first hired in my current position, I encountered a lot of opposition for many different reasons. Things began to progress so badly on my job that I honestly thought that I had made a huge mistake in accepting the position. I spent many nights crying after work and every morning I dreaded going into the office. When things began to negatively escalate, I made the decision to fast and to pray in order for me to maintain my composure and to maintain lucid thinking. During my time of fasting and praying the Lord told me that He was going to turn things around. A few months later He did just that and I went from being the "underdog," so to speak, to being recognized as an

Associate of the month and assigned to mentor new hires in my department.

During the process, my boss, who is a Christian, was experiencing major physical challenges. She desired a closer and deeper walk with Christ and God would allow us to discuss the things of God. Many times I would share with her in scripture, words of encouragement or prayer. She touched my heart one day when she said that she was a better person because of me.

I believe that God allowed me to be hired to help pray my boss through the tough times that she was facing. She consented for me to have my prayer group pray for her deliverance and recovery as well. I truly believe the warfare that I experienced when I first started the job was the work of Satan to prevent me from seeing the need to intercede for a fellow sister in Christ. When I turned my plate down to fast and pray, the scales fell from my eyes and I realized that this job was more than me just getting a paycheck, but about being available to minister to the needs of others.

Who has God assigned you to help on your job? Perhaps you have been asking God to open up doors for you to minister on a public platform and you have failed to realize that ministry opportunities avail themselves to you on a daily basis amongst your coworkers. Your assignment may not necessarily be to go "preach Jesus" to a coworker, but to earnestly intercede on their behalf for their salvation,

WHY do you want God to use you??

peace of mind and deliverance. Intercessory prayer is a powerful life changing ministry that should not be overlooked or underplayed.

Ministry Motives

As previously mentioned, I am a firm believer that we are all called to some level of specialized ministry or service for the advancement of the Kingdom of God. The bible provides us with examples in both the old and New Testament scriptures of women operating in ministerial capacities. Examples of such are:

Old Testament:
Deborah
The only female judge in Israel
(Judges 4:4)

Miriam
Was a prophetess
(Exodus 15:20)
Rahab
Acted as a protector for Joshua and the spies
(Joshua 2)

Ruth
Was a Mother in Zion.
She birthed Obed who was King David's grandfather
whose lineage Christ was born through
(Ruth 4)

Hannah
Was an Intercessor and a worshipper
(I Samuel 1:9-19)

Abigail
Had the gift of Wisdom which caused the life of her household
to be spared
(I Samuel 25:3-32)

Esther
An intercessor saving her people from annihilation
(Read entire book of Esther)

New Testament:
Samaritan Woman
Acted as an Evangelist upon hearing the Word of the Lord
Many came to Christ through her testimony.
(John 4:9-39)

Martha
Was a servant
Luke (10:40)

Mary (sister of Martha)
Was a worshipper
(Luke 10:40-41)
Tabitha (aka Dorcas)
Was a missionary
(Acts 9:36)

Rhoda
A young girl of great faith
(Acts 12:13)

Phebe
Had the gift of hospitality. Assisted many
(Romans 16:1-2)

Based on this list you should feel assured that the tug that you feel in your heart towards ministry is valid. God has always used women to help get His agenda fulfilled. However, I want to challenge you regarding this "call to ministry" that you are experiencing.

I hear a lot of women make the comment, "I know that I'm called to ministry," or "I really want God to use me." I myself have made these comments many times. However, as I pondered these statements, I began to wonder whether or not we really comprehend what ministry entails. To those who are waiting for ministry "opportunities," let me propose the following questions to you..."

- ✓ Why do you want to minister?
- ✓ Do you understand that when you enter into the ministry, you are willingly opening yourself up to public ridicule, criticism, spiritual warfare, and/or the monopolization of your time and resources?

These are typical accompaniments to ministry. Ministry is not a glamorous Hollywood experience, nor is it an easy road to walk. It requires much tears and much sacrifice. Are you really spiritually prepared for the challenge?

In the church of today, the term "ministry" is used very loosely. Many of us tend to think about televangelists who preach before crowds of thousands, have a popular "fan bases," drive fancy cars, live in mansions, and receive hefty financial pay-outs. True, some have been blessed to experience these gains as a result of operating in ministry. However, if our motives for operating in ministry are to replicate these results, than our motives are misplaced. Our main objective for operating in the ministry of the Lord should be to win souls to Christ...period. It should not be about self-validation, financial gain, or anything that points to us as opposed to pointing to the cross. When Jesus ministered for 3 ½ years on the earth, he maintained the attitude of "being about His father's business." **(See Luke 2:49)**. He never made it about him gaining the approval of the crowd or promoting himself…He always promoted the Kingdom of God.

When our motive is to genuinely see souls saved and added to the Kingdom of God, then we can expect figuratively/and or naturally for our lives to look more like the Apostle Paul. The Apostle Paul, who was the greatest missionary second to Christ, described the effects of operating in ministry as **such (II Corinthians 11:23-27) NLT:** *"Are they servants of Christ? I know I sound like a madman, but I have served him far more! I have worked harder, been put in prison more often, been whipped times without number, and faced death again and again.* [24]

Five different times the Jewish leaders gave me thirty-nine lashes. [25]

Three times I was beaten with rods. Once I was stoned. Three times I was shipwrecked. Once I spent a whole night and a day adrift at sea. [26]

I have travelled on many long journeys. I have faced danger from rivers and from robbers. I have faced danger from my own people, the Jews, as well as from the Gentiles. I have faced danger in the cities, in the deserts, and on the seas. And I have faced danger from men who claim to be believers but are not.[27]

I have worked hard and long, enduring many sleepless nights. I have been hungry and thirsty and have often gone without food. I have shivered in the cold, without enough clothing to keep me warm".

Are you ready for the challenges of REAL ministry?

After reading Apostle Paul's account of his ministry exploits...are you still anxious and excited about ministry? Paul's circumstances were extreme, but depending on what Christ has called us to individually, they may not be unrealistic. The point that I am attempting to make is that in order to truly embrace ministry, we must embrace the reality of suffering and tribulation. If you are convinced that the call of God is upon your life to operate in the ministry of the Word and deliverance, than I urge you to heed the advice of the Apostle Paul: to "Wait on our Ministering" **(Romans 12:7).** When we wait on our ministry to be developed, it will allow us time to become rooted and grounded in the things of God. When we are rooted and grounded in the faith **(see Colossians 12:3)** we will not make the name of our Lord ashamed.

Let Us Selah and Pray

"Dear Lord, I come before you and place all of my heart and its motives on the altar. I desire to be used by You and to operate in the things that you have called me to. However, I want to be sure that my motives are right and pure in your sight. Help me to realize that my ultimate purpose and goal is to honor Your name by winning souls to You. The ministry that You have given me is not about me, but it is completely about You and enlarging your Kingdom. Please anoint me afresh. Help me not to operate in my flesh or become distracted with silly things such as competing or comparing what you have called me to do with what you have called others to do. Give me a heart to pray even for the ministries of my fellow brothers and sisters in Christ. Lord, help me not to make You ashamed in anyway. I pray these things in Jesus' name, amen."

Ministry Assignments

Once we have done a "motive check" and determined that our ministry goals are pure before the Lord, we must begin to prepare ourselves to walk in the assignment.

Have you ACCEPTED your assignment?

The assignment is the specific task or position that God has called us to individually. It can be short-term, long-term, or lifelong. It can be multifaceted assignment(s) such as operating as an intercessor, pastor, and teacher or just one assignment (i.e.: operating solely as an intercessor) that we are called to. Whatever the assignment may be, we must recognize it, embrace it, prepare for it, and begin to operate in it. Note that each one of us has an assignment to complete. Regardless of the assignments complexity or breadth, each and every assignment in the Kingdom is equally important in the sight of God. All of us uniquely make up the Body of Christ **(see I Corinthians 12:12-27)**.

Some of us know our assignments and are comfortable operating in them. Others are still searching and uncertain about exactly what she should be doing.

Discovering our assignments takes time, patience, prayer, discernment, and godly counsel. Personally speaking, portions of the ministry that God has given to me, such as preaching and teaching the Word was made known to me from my childhood. I always loved to read and listen to the Word of God and ministering from it always flowed naturally for me. However, other aspects of my ministry have only been revealed to me in recent years. For example, I have finally accepted the fact that I have an anointing on my life to specifically minister to the needs of women across all age groups. My call to women's ministry was actually birthed out of the many bad choices, mistakes, and struggles that I had experienced over the years. Once I stopped lamenting over the negative aspects of my life and submitted them to the Lord, He began to cause opportunities for me to minister from them. The Lord taught me to stop beating myself up about past poor judgment calls, but to allow Him to build a platform for me to minister to others struggling with similar issues.

Self-discovery is one of the most effective ways to tap into God's purpose for our lives. We must search our hearts deeply for what we feel most drawn to and what we are most passionate about it. For example, I can guarantee that if you discover that you lack patience and tolerance with youth, and you become increasingly annoyed when they are in your presence, you are probably not called to operate in youth ministry. Likewise, if you find great joy in sharing the Gospel with the elderly, the incapacitated, and/ or the disenfranchised, you would probably do well working in some branch of missions ministry.

Once we have identified our passion, we must make it a daily matter of fasting and prayer. Please understand that ministry is not all about preaching and teaching the Word of God. Ministry encompasses hospitality, giving, intercessory prayer, and so much more! The following scriptures list a variety of spiritual gifts that are in operation in the body of Christ:

Romans 12:6-8

1 Corinthians 12:4-11

1 Corinthians 12:28

Ephesians 4:11-13

As we begin to fast and pray about what God wants for us to do, we should expect Him to give us confirmation concerning it. His confirmation can come in a variety of ways. He can cause us to read a magazine article about the very area of ministry that we had been praying about, or He can cause a preacher to speak from the very same subject matter. We must learn how to allow our spiritual hearing to be sharpened so that we do not miss God's voice when He is using various vessels to deliver His words of confirmation to us.

Once we have discovered what our assignment is, we must be keenly aware that God expects us to complete it. He does not issue assignments to us for us to toss them aside or allow them to collect "shelf dust." When He reveals His will to us, we are responsible for walking in it.

I would not recommend resisting the will of God. Bad things tend to happen when we blatantly ignore and refuse to do what God has commissioned us to do. The prophet Jonah is a prime example of the consequences associated with avoiding God given assignments. Let's take a look at Jonah's experience with failing to accept his assignment.

The Scriptures teach us, in **Jonah 1: 1-3,** that God had commissioned the Prophet Jonah to travel to the city of Nineveh and to proclaim the message of repentance to its residents. Jonah, however, did not like this particular assignment, so he made a conscious decision to head in the opposite direction of where God told him to go. Jonah did not realize it at the time, but he was making a terrible decision by rejecting his assignment.

As the story unfolds, God teaches Jonah first hand that when He issues an assignment He expects compliance, and when His expectations go unmet, grave consequences follow. God allowed Jonah to literally be swallowed up by a big fish that held him captive for three days and three nights in its belly. Can you imagine being swallowed alive by a fish and having to live inside it along with everything else it digested? He ended up living among carcasses, dredge, and waste because he rejected God's call upon his life. It seems to me that he would have lived far more comfortably and with far less drama if he would have just obeyed God.

Are you living in the "belly of a fish" for failure to obey God?

Sometimes in life we find ourselves in a similar situation as Jonah. We find ourselves in a dark and scary place in life where we feel a void of God's presence. We wonder, "How did I end up here." Many times we ended up in these places as a result of failing to do the will of God.

After three days and three nights of living among waste in the belly of the fish, Jonah finally came to himself and repented for wasting time and disobeying God. The bible declares that upon his release from the belly of the fish, he made the three-day journey to Nineveh in just one day. That one experience put a "pep in his step" to fulfil the will of God for his life. Perhaps you have found yourself in the "belly of life," and you want to get out. I urge you to do as Jonah did, repent, and get in a hurry to do what God has told you to do!

There are many reasons why we drag our feet when it comes to walking in the call of God for our lives. Some of us are not convinced about the call of God upon our lives, and we struggle with zeroing in on what He would have for us to do. Then, there are those amongst us who struggle with feelings of unworthiness and inadequacies at being used by God due to our past failures and mistakes. Lastly, there are those of us who have suffered such great abuse, neglect, and abandonment in our past that it has crippled us from giving God a complete "yes."

What is holding you back from completing your assignment? My dear sister, only you can answer that question. I encourage you to come clean with God in prayer and to allow Him to minister back into your spirit. Coming clean with God about what holds you back may require you to pull up painful memories and release them to Him. It may require you to forgive all those who have left you, hurt you, and let you down. Whatever it takes, you must identify the clog in the drain that blocks the flow of God in your life. The time is now to accept your assignment and to begin to walk in it. **Remember this: your failure to obey God and complete your assignment results in holding up someone else's deliverance. I do not want to be responsible for prolonging someone's prison sentence, knowing that I possess the key to their freedom. How about you?**

Let Us Selah and Pray

"Dear Lord, I come to You today seeking You for the assignment that You have placed on my life. Please help me to know with assurance what I should be doing and help me to develop a strategy to complete the assignment. Kind Father, please forgive me for where I have resisted your will in the

past, where I have run away from the call of God upon my life, and have made a myriad of excuses for operating in disobedience. Where I have procrastinated and simply been lazy, Lord, I'm sorry. Lord, where failure to do Your will has caused me to end up in a low spiritual place where I cannot feel Your love and protection, Lord I repent. I cry out to you as King David did, "Create in me a clean heart and renew within me a right spirit. Cast me not away from thy presence and take not your holy spirit away from me." **(Psalms 51).** *Lord, if You give me another chance, I'll take it. Lord, I yield all of my insecurities, sins, and past failures to You. If You are willing to use me, then I am willing to be used by You. I thank You for restoration. I thank You for a fresh start. I thank You most of all for choosing me above all the women of the earth to do this for You. I trust You and I am willing to do all that you say. In Jesus' name, amen."*

Chapter 5

The Gift of Money

Ecclesiastes 10:19
The Message (MSG)

"Laughter and bread go together, And wine gives sparkle to life – But it's money that makes the world go around."

"Show me the money" is a famous line spoken by the fictional character Rod Tidwell in the 1996 sports drama, "Jerry Maguire." I would think that most of the women reading this book would not mind being shown just a little more

SHOW ME THE MONEY!!

money in their pay checks, bank accounts, trust funds, 401K, or wallets. After all, our opening scripture states it best, *"It's money that makes the world go round."* The reality is that we need money. However, as Christian women, we need to understand how we should handle this resource from a biblical perspective. If we manage our money God's way, He will in turn "show us the money" in abundance.

Let's establish the fact that the desire to have money is not a sin. *I Timothy 6:10 states: "For the love of money is the root of all evil: which while some coveted after, they have erred from the faith, and pierced themselves through with many sorrows."*

We are not to love money, become obsessed with obtaining it, become depressed by being void of it, or invest our faith or hope in it. However, we must accept the reality that money is a needed resource that God blesses us with for our living comfort.

As punishment for his sin in the Garden of Eden, God warned Adam that if he wanted to eat, he would be required to work. *(Genesis 3:19).* As reward for his work, man would receive some form of payment in which he would be able to trade to purchase his food and to provide for his living accommodations. Money is a necessary part of life. If we honor God with this resource that He has blessed us with, He will anoint it to increase and to multiply.

What does the Bible have to say about money? Quite a bit. It teaches us that we should:

- ✓ Honor God with our money through tithing and offering

- ✓ *Avoid occurring debt as much as possible and embrace a spirit of being a lender*

- ✓ Save money

- ✓ Give to others

Before we proceed, I am compelled to share with you that proper money management has been a weakness in my life. Failure to properly honor God in all things, and just being plain irresponsible and presumptuous caused me to make a myriad of financial blunders. The good news about my experience is that I've learned from them and am now in a position to instruct others, including my son, on how to avoid the pitfalls that I entered into. I truly believe that if we apply the wisdom of **Proverbs 3:5-6 which** states, *"Trust in the* LORD *with all thine heart; and lean not unto thine own understanding. In all thy ways acknowledge him, and he shall direct thy paths,"* to how we handle our money, we will begin to see a continuous flow of financial gain and increase. Let's take a didactic look at each of the topics listed above and the instructions that the bible provides to us.

Tithing and Offering

TITHE

The principle of tithing dates back to the Old Testament beginning with **Genesis 14:20** with Abraham tithing to the high priest, Melchizdek. What is tithing?

Tithing in its most simplistic definition is the act of presenting God with the FIRST 10 percent of all our INCREASE.

10% BELONGS to God!

Proverbs 3:9 teaches us to:

"Honour the Lord with thy substance and with the first fruits of all thine increase."

There are two terms in this text that warrants extraction and further discussion. They are *"honour"* and *"first fruits."*

Honour

The term "honour" in this verse refers to the act of paying homage, worship, great respect, and/or regard to. Based on this definition we learn that tithing is actually a form of worship.

Giving is a form of WORSHIP!

We have been blessed with the privilege of worshipping God and showing Him how much we respect and highly regard His divine provision to us by presenting Him with a tenth of all that He allows us to earn. Since tithing is a form of worship, we must be mindful of our attitude and our disposition in presenting it to Him. We ought not to present our tithe to God begrudgingly or regard it as an annoying bill that must be paid in order to avoid the curse of God.

I have been taught the basic principles of tithing from my childhood. However, in retrospect, I was never taught to respect tithes as a form of worship. I tithed because I feared being "cursed with a curse" as recorded in *Malachi 3:9*. True, failure to present God with the tithe will yield a curse. However, I am learning that my attitude in my presentation to Him is also important.

For example, there have been times in my life that I gave my tithe but I did not do it with joy. I did it out of obligation and with a spirit of reluctance. I forgot that "God loves a cheerful giver," as recorded in *II Corinthians 9:8*. Because God is a keeper of His Word, He has always adequately provided for my family's needs as well as some of our wants simply because I was obedient in giving my tithe. However, I am convinced that I have not experienced the fullness of His blessings because my attitude was not right in how I presented the tithe to Him. I truly believe that if we adopt an attitude of worship and thankfulness when we tithe, we will experience the Lord "*pouring out a blessing so great that we won't have room enough to take it in"* as He promised in **Malachi 3:10(B) NLT.**

God is offended when we do not bring his tithe to Him. When we withhold our tithe, He views us as cheaters and releases a curse on us. **(See *Malachi 3:8-9*).** Why is He offended? He is offended because we are robbing Him of worship and thanksgiving that is due to Him! We must remember that God created us to worship Him! When He does not receive our worship, it kindles His anger.

First fruits

The www.freedictionary defines first fruits as *"The first gathered fruit of a harvest, offered to God in gratitude."* Our first fruit, in modern times, would be the very first check we write, or payment that we make when we receive any form of financial increase. God wants His portion FIRST, with a spirit of GRATITUDE, before we begin to allocate our money to any other resource. This means that we ought not to pay all of our bills FIRST and then write out our tithe check LAST. God wants us to honor the tithe by making it a

God wants His cut FIRST!

priority over our mortgage, rent, childcare, groceries, cell phone, and other payments.

<u>OFFERING</u>

We must also be reminded that God expects us to present Him with an offering in **ADDITION** to our tithe according to *Malachi 3:8*. An offering in the Old Testament represented a sacrifice or a gift presented to God. Today, we can also view our offerings to God as a sacrifice or a gift to present to Him as thankfulness for His many blessings. Note, the quoted scripture does not indicate the amount of offering that we should present to God, but we should be aware that God always expects us to do our very best. Ladies, God pays attention to our offering, so we should not be stingy or give with a negative attitude. Two examples of women in the bible offering God their best are indicated below.

The Widow's Offering

Mark 12:41-43 provides a beautiful illustration of how God not only pays attention to our offerings, but He pays attention to

God SEES us when we give!!

the spirit in which we give our offering. In this text,

Jesus is sitting near the collection plate and he is WATCHING as rich people dropped large amounts into it. As he is WATCHING, a poor widow drops in two coins. Jesus comments to His disciples that this woman's offering was far more valuable than the rich people because she gave all that she had with a heart of genuineness and gratitude.

We learn from this widow woman that when we give our offering to God, we must give with the understanding that God is looking. It does not matter if the Pastor or the Bishop sees us. We want God to take notice and be pleased. Also, we learn that we should never be embarrassed if we only have a small amount to give. That being said, please stop balling and folding up your $1, $5, or $10 bill(s) if that is genuinely all that you have to give in the public offering! Give it with joy and gratitude and God will take notice and bless you accordingly.

The Alabaster Box

Matthew 26:6-10 provides us with another awesome depiction of the power of giving. The unnamed woman in this text is the exact opposite of the poor widow woman. This woman had access to wealth.

This scripture records that she approached Jesus while he was eating at Simon's house and poured expensive perfume over his head out of a beautiful alabaster box. Her offering to Christ touched Him so deeply that he proclaimed this woman's international and historical fame! Now THAT was an offering. Can you imagine giving to God with such sincerity that you it promotes you to international and historical recognition? This woman had a lot and she gave it with sincerity.

Perhaps we need to adjust and fine tune our attitude towards bringing our tithe and offering to Christ. The time is now for us to change our approach to giving so that we may experience the fullness of God's blessings and provisions.

Let Us Selah and Pray

"Dear Lord, I come before you to give you thanks for your divine provision for me and my family. Where I have failed to tithe and give my offering properly and faithfully in accordance to your Word, I repent. Where I have given my tithe and offering with the wrong disposition, I also ask you to forgive me. Lord, please change my attitude toward tithes and offering and cause me to see bringing it to you as a privilege

and an honor and not as a burden or a bill. Touch my heart that I would always bring my financial gifts to you with thanksgiving and joy.

"As I become fully obedient to your Word, I ask that you would remember your Word to me. Please pour me out a blessing so great that I won't have room enough to receive it. Lord, the scripture encourages us to test you to see whether or not you will be faithful to us in blessing us if we are faithful in giving our tithe and offering. Lord, I accept the challenge of bringing all that is due to you unto you. I accept your Word and I expect to receive the promised increase, in Jesus' name, amen."

Avoiding Debt

Now that we have embraced the concept of proper tithing and offering, we are now one step closer to being *"shown the money."* The next topic that we shall tackle is "debt avoidance."

Financial debt, to my chagrin, is a familiar topic to me. As I stated in the opening of this chapter, financial management has not been my strong suit and I have found myself

DEBT IS NOT OF GOD!!!

struggling with debt over the years. As I have matured, I

realize that a lot of my poor financial choices were based in a lack of wisdom, knowledge and patience. Thankfully, God has been quite merciful to my family and myself, and has allowed us to maneuverer through some financial challenges.

Let us establish that it is not the will of God for his people to be burned by the curse of debt. There are many scriptures that encourage debt-free living beginning in the book of Deuteronomy. **Deuteronomy 15:5-6** records a promise that God made to Israel pending their obedience to all of his commandments. He promised them that they would be in a position to lend to many nations and would not have to borrow if they remained faithful unto Him. The Apostle Paul continues the teaching on debt-free living in **Romans 13:8** when he admonishes the people to, *"Owe nothing to anyone-except for you obligation to love one another."*

What do we do if we find ourselves in debt? Let's establish the fact that it is not the end of the world and the mercy of God is available to help us to navigate through it. The first step in breaking free from the curse of debt is to understand how we ended up in the situation in the first place. The second step is to identify the root cause of the problem, such as living outside of our means, lack of restraint, shopping addictions, and/or generational curses. Once the root cause of the problem is revealed, we need to repent for not being good stewards over our finances and then we need to develop a strategy to tackle the debt and to avoid repeating the behavior. This will require more than prayer. It will require financial counselling and a change in our spending behaviors.

As with any addiction or destructive behavior, I am a firm believer, that the debt struggles can be a generational occurrence. I will use myself as an example. In her younger years, my mother struggled with a shopping addiction and in turn incurred huge amounts of debt. Thankfully, she was eventually delivered from her struggle, but I truly believe that I inherited it. I, by no means, blame my problems over the years on my mother, but I do acknowledge the fact that I mimicked the behavior in my own life. In order to break free from this generational curse, I have had to acknowledge it to God, confess it to others, repent, and change my behavior and attitude toward money and spending. Likewise, I have had to clench my teeth and prepare for the long haul of paying my way out of debt. It is not easy, but it's worth it in the end to be able to live without the burden of debt hanging over my head on a daily basis.

We should note that God expects us to do our best to pay what we owe. He is a merciful God, and I know that He will provide us with the assistance that we need in order to do right by our creditors. He is a miracle worker, and could completely eradicate our debt; however, our mind-set should be that if we borrow, then we should pay it back. We do not want to be counted among the evildoers! **Psalms 37:1(A)** states, *"The wicked borrow and never repay!"*

Saving Money

The bible not only discourages incurring debt, but it also encourages us to adopt an attitude of saving a portion of all of our income. If we embrace the concept of saving money, we can expect God to show us more, and more money! **Proverbs 6:8 (NLT)** describes how the ant labors hard all summer gathering food in preparation for the coming winter. Winter, in my opinion, represents the seasons of life when growth and opportunities are scarce. Savers, however, do not have to be afraid of the winter because they prepared for it in anticipation of its arrival!

Short-term and Long-term Savings

We should earnestly seek to establish short term savings as well as long-term savings plans. Short-term savings is money that we can immediately access in case of emergencies. Should vehicle or major appliances break down, uninsured medical needs arise, travel expenses, or any other type of unexpected situations arise, we will be able to address them without the need to borrow from anyone because we have already set money aside. Long-term savings, such as 401K plans, IRA, or other investment portfolios will help us to live comfortably when we are blessed to retire.

Leaving an Inheritance

The last point that I want to discuss is developing a savings plan for our children and grandchildren. This is a biblical concept that is addressed in **Proverbs 13:22** which states: "*Good people leave an inheritance to their grandchildren, but the sinner's wealth passes to the godly.*" With the instability in our economic climate, our society recognizes the need to provide financial security for our offspring. Educational plans such as a 529 is an example of an inexpensive and simple savings option that is available to prepare for our children's future educational provision and security.

Likewise, I'm a firm believer in life insurance. Many companies provide free life insurance benefits to their full/-time employees. However, I am of the mindset that supplemental life insurance should be purchased in the event of job loss. Life insurance will not only provide for our family with the finances to cover our funeral expenses, but will also provide for them to live comfortably after our transition to heaven.

Are you are an "ant" or are you a "raccoon"? An ant's perspective is to save as much as possible to ensure future provision. A raccoon, on the other hand, ravages through all it has access to and makes a complete mess. I've made the decision to become more "ant-like" and leave my "raccoon lifestyle" behind me. I desire to have access to all that God is willing to give to me. However, I

ARE YOU AN ANT OR ARE YOU A RACOON??

realize that in order for Him to release more to me, then I must be willing to be a good steward over all of His provision. The same holds true for you as well.

Giving to Others

I believe that God is truly going to show us the money. However, He is not going to do it for our benefit alone, but for us to be a blessing to others. *John 3:16* is one of my favorite scriptures. It provides a beautiful illustration of giving as sign of love and concern for others. It states: *"For God so loved the world, that he gave his only begotten Son, that whosoever believeth in him should not perish, but have everlasting life."*

God unselfishly gave the most valuable possession that He had for the sake of our future, the life of his precious Son, Jesus Christ. He **Pray for a spirit of Generosity!** displayed His concern through the act of giving. We, too, must show our concern by unselfishly giving to those in need. *Proverbs 19:17* states: *"He that hath pity upon the poor lendeth unto the LORD; and that which he hath given will he pay him again"*.

We do not have to be afraid or reluctant to give to others in need. When we give to the needy, it is equivalent to giving directly to God. When we give to God, we can rest assured that He will pay us back with interest!

Let Us Selah and Pray

"Dear Jesus, Proverbs 3:6 teaches us that in all of our ways we should acknowledge you and you would direct our paths. Help me to realize that this includes the way that I manage the money that you allow me to possess. Where I may have failed in the past by not properly tithing and giving you the offering that you require and deserve, I repent and I ask that you would forgive me. Help me to develop the faith that I need to tithe properly and consistently.

Lord, I commit the 90% of the rest of the financial increase that you have allotted to me into your hand. I ask that you would give me the wisdom and knowledge that I need to be a good steward over it. Where I have not been a good steward in the past, and I am guilty of being wasteful, I genuinely repent and I ask for your forgiveness. Please give me a heart of a saver. Please give me a heart of a giver. I ask for your direction in paying off any and all debts that I have incurred. Give me a heart to do right by my creditors and to pay them what I owe to them. Once I have paid them off, help me not to incur any additional debt. Lord, I rebuke and I bind up generational curses of poverty and debt that I am battling. I speak the Word over my finances that you have assigned me to the lender and not the borrower according to Deuteronomy 15. Likewise, I bring every one of my thoughts regarding my ability to be financially successful into your obedience according to *2 Corinthians 10:5, in Jesus' name. God, I thank you for blessing my money as I surrender its use to your wisdom and guidance. I thank you for prospering it and showing me how to make it multiply, in Jesus' name, Amen."*

Conclusion

Women of God, we are special and we are important to God. We mean more to God than what our minds can comprehend. He loves us so much that He gave the best that He had for us...that being the life of His only beloved Son, Jesus Christ **(see John 3:16)** to die on the cross for our redemption. The only thing that he asks for us in return is to offer Him our most prized possession....that being our heart. If we commit all the desires, concerns, fears, insecurities, struggles, and decisions into the hands of our capable God, we can rest assured that our futures will be secured and established.

Ladies, we have to learn how to delight, or find great pleasure in who God is. When we take pleasure in His sovereignty, omniscience, and omnipresence, His Word promises us that He will give us the desires of our heart **(see Psalms 37:4).** We don't have to stress or worry about our future. Our future is secure if we just learn to delight ourselves in the Lord.

****Let Us Selah and Pray****

"Dear Lord, we thank You for the great concern that You have for all women. We are grateful that You are keenly aware of not only our needs, but our desires as well. Lord, please teach us how to simply find pleasure in knowing that

You have all aspects of our lives under control. Help us to stop worrying and stressing about the future. Help us to embrace a spirit of peace, contentment, and joy in knowing that You are sitting on the throne of our hearts. We thank You for the confirmation that You see us and that You know us intimately. We thank You that we are not forgotten, but You remember every single detail of our lives, even down to the number of hairs on our head according to **Luke 12:7.** *What a mighty God You are! Lord, today is a new day for us. No longer will we submit to worry, defeat, or fear. We bind up, in the name of Jesus, every spirit that would make us be fretful about our future! Instead, we embrace the spirit of* **Philippians 4:6** *and make the decision today to not worry about anything, but to pray about everything that we need and to give You thanks for what You have already done! Lord, if we do this, Your Word says that will experience YOUR peace which exceeds anything that we can understand. It's a new day for us! We commit our hearts, minds, bodies and spirits to you! We know that they are in good hands, in Jesus' name, AMEN."*

Our Daily Affirmation

(Based on Philippians 4:6)

I WILL not worry about anything today, but I WILL pray about everything.

I WILL tell God what I need and I WILL thank Him for what he has already done.

I WILL experience GOD'S PEACE today which exceed any and all of my circumstances.

God's peace WILL guard my heart and my mind in Christ Jesus!

HEART OF A WOMAN: MOTHERHOOD, MARRIAGE, MINISTRY, AND MONEY

[i]Madeline Vann, MPH. "Physical Health, Emotional Health: Connecting the Dots." *Www.everdayhealth.com.* Everyday Health, 22 Dec. 2009. Web. 01 Jan. 2016. <http://www.everydayhealth.com/emotional-health/connecting-dots.aspx>.